# Aquatics:
# A Revived Approach
# to Pediatric Management

# Aquatics: A Revived Approach to Pediatric Management

Faye H. Dulcy, Editor

The Haworth Press
New York

*Aquatics: A Revived Approach to Pediatric Management* has also been published as *Physical & Occupational Therapy in Pediatrics,* Volume 3, Number 1, Spring 1983.

The Haworth Press, Inc., 10 Alice Street, Binghamton, NY 13904–1580

Library of Congress Cataloging in Publication Data
Main entry under title:

Aquatics, a revived approach to pediatric management.

"Aquatics, a revived approach to pediatric management has also been published as Physical and occupational therapy in pediatrics, volume 3, number 1, spring 1983"—Verso t.p.
   Includes bibliographical references.
   1. Aquatic exercises—Therapeutic use. 2. Exercise therapy for children. 3. Physically handicapped children—Rehabilitation. I. Dulcy, Faye H. [DNLM: 1. Hydrotherapy—In infancy and childhood. WI PH683P v.3 no. 1 / WB 520 A656]
RJ53.A68A68 1983          615.8'53          83-85
ISBN 0-86656-215-X

# Aquatics:
# A Revived Approach
# to Pediatric Management

Physical & Occupational Therapy in Pediatrics
Volume 3, Number 1

## CONTENTS

# ANNOTATED BIBLIOGRAPHY

Aquatics for Disabled Persons

*Susan M. Attermeier, MACT, LPT*
*Faye H. Dulcy, MMSc, RPT*
*Susan R. Harris, PhD, RPT*
*Karen Martin, RPT*

MARILYN SEIF, MS, *Speech Pathologist, Marshfield Clinic, Marshfield, WI*

GEORGIA M. SHAMBES, PhD, *Professor, Program in Physical Therapy, School of Allied Health Professions, University of Wisconsin-Madison*

EARL SIEGEL, MD, *Professor of Maternal and Child Health; Clinical Professor of Pediatrics, University of North Carolina at Chapel Hill*

NAPOLEON WOLANSKI, PhD, DSc, *Head, Department of Human Ecology of the Polish Academy of Sciences, Warsaw, Poland*

# Foreword

All the authors of this issue of *Physical & Occupational Therapy in Pediatrics* are extremely pleased to be able to devote an entire issue to an area which we are all very excited about—aquatic programs for children. In our literature searches and our research, we have found that, except for the classic hydrotherapy articles,[1-4] very little literature is authored by American health professionals. Instead, aquatic professionals, recreational therapists, or United Kingdom health professionals have provided the current aquatic program literature. In this issue, we hope to illuminate aquatics as a viable treatment and educational technique for pediatric therapists by presenting the problems we see existing in aquatics, a theoretical model, research, and clinical applications of aquatic programming.

This aquatic theme issue came together through the enthusiasm of the authors and the excitement we found in sharing our perspectives with each other. We also share general feelings that either far too few therapists are using aquatics as a media in the first place, or those who are using aquatics cleverly and uniquely are not sharing it with other clinicians and students. Our rationale in developing a theme issue is, therefore, to begin filling some of the gaps in therapeutic aquatic literature and practice.

In the first article of this issue, the guest editor outlines problems existing in the literature and practice from which the need for a framework for designing and implementing aquatic programs was identified. The guest editor next describes the theoretical model and guidelines which were designed and validated as a transdisciplinary, developmental, aquatic approach for disabled children. This Integrated Recreational and Therapeutic Model and Guidelines were approved by consensus of a panel of multidisciplinary experts and are presented as a basis for the following works in the issue.

All the papers which follow may be considered clinical and research applications of the developmental theoretical model. The clinical and research applications are presented in developmental order, starting with premature infants and progressing to adolescents. Jane Sweeney presents research on the effects of using aquatic treatment in the intensive care nursery. As in the model, the therapist cooperatively works with the parents and unit nurses, as well as with the infant. He or she examines the physiological changes resulting from treatment, and uses the water to affect tone and state in the infant. Additionally, aquatics is a media used to facilitate the transfer of parental learning about bathing and handling from the nursery to the home setting.

Susan Attermeier discusses a case study involving bringing the aquatic environment into the clinic in order to enhance the positive results obtained in the pool and at bath time. The water enhances developmental progressions of normalizing posture and tone, utilizing the environmental considerations of the water, as identified in the model. In this case, Ms. Attermeier integrates the Neurodevelopmental Treatment (NDT) and Rood approaches to treatment with aquatics.

Karen Martin presents a preschool program in which parental involvement is a vital part. Preschoolers having various disabilities learn water safety skills as well as integrate some specially designed exercises into their aquatic training. Recreational and therapeutic staff work together with parents in the transdisciplinary method as is also described in the model.

The last article is a description of an application of aquatics to a specific population of severely and profoundly disabled. A model program is presented by Susan Harris and Marie Thompson for using aquatics as a cross-environmental treatment and educational approach to facilitate the development of gross motor skills with deaf-blind adolescents.

Finally, several books and articles pertinent to aquatics are reviewed by the authors of this issue, and an annotated bibliography is presented.

*Faye H. Dulcy, MMSc, RPT*
*Guest Editor*

## REFERENCES

1. Kolb ME: Principles of underwater exercise. *Physical Therapy Review* 37: 1336-1365, 1957.
2. Lowman CL: Therapeutic indications for pool therapy. *Physical Therapy Review* 37: 224, 1957.
3. Lowman CL, Roen SG: *Therapeutic Use of Pools and Tanks.* Philadelphia, WB Saunders Co., 1952.
4. Stewart, JB: Exercise in Water, in Lichts S (ed): *Therapeutic Exercise.* Baltimore, Waverly Press, Inc., 1965.

# Aquatics:
# A Revived Approach
# to Pediatric Management

# Aquatic Programs for Disabled Children: An Overview and an Analysis of the Problems

Faye H. Dulcy, MMSc, RPT

**ABSTRACT.** Unidisciplinary *recreational* and *therapeutic* approaches to aquatic programs for the disabled have created an apparent dichotomy which carries with it associated programmatic problems. The *recreational/therapeutic* split exists in both practice and literature and a probably influential relationship is demonstrated between program type and philosophies, principles, staff composition, roles and training. The purpose of this article is to analyze these issues, as well as to describe an *integrated* recreational and therapeutic approach to aquatic programming, which is proposed as a solution and a rationale for development of a model and guidelines for aquatic intervention for disabled children.

## INTRODUCTION: THE DICHOTOMY IN APPROACHES TO AQUATIC PROGRAMMING

A dichotomy, rather than an integration, seems to exist between recreational and therapeutic aquatic approaches to pediatric treatment in both the literature and in current practice. The dichotomy prevails throughout program philosophy and principles, composition and roles of program staff, and their methods and training. The resulting programs are thus unidisciplinary and are not adequate to comprehensively use the capacities or meet the needs of the disabled or delayed pediatric population.

The purposes of this article are to delineate three types of aquatic programs, the problems or discrepancies between the parts of each program type and an idealized integrated approach, and to identify the contributions of each program type to that ideal. The three types of programs, their philosophies, principles and related problems are described. Addi-

Faye H. Dulcy is presently Assistant Professor in the Department of Physical Therapy, School of Allied Health, Texas Tech University Health Sciences Center, Lubbock, TX 79430. She received her certificate and Bachelor of Science degree from Northwestern University. This article is an excerpt from her master's thesis, done in partial fulfillment for the Masters of Medical Science degree at Emory University, Atlanta, Georgia.

*1*

tional problems are created secondarily as a result of the distinctive approaches to composition, roles and training of program staff. These may be considered the weaknesses of each unidisciplinary approach which cause inefficiency. These differences and resulting problems and weaknesses illustrate the discrepancies from the ideal and support the need for a counter-proposal to complete the integrated approach. On the other hand the specialized methods are, in fact, the strengths of each approach and are necessary contributions to an integrated approach.

The identified gaps between present unidisciplinary programs and an ideal, realized to be an integrated approach, were used as rationales for the development of a theoretical model and guidelines for aquatic programs. Analyses of this existing dichotomy in aquatic programs, and the problems inherent in a non-integrated model have not been previously made, and were prerequisites to the development and validation of an ideal *integrated model* and guidelines to be discussed in the second article to follow.

Water is used as a recreational and therapeutic medium by two distinctly different groups of professional people, usually for two different purposes. Various types of aquatic programs for disabled children have long been available. Recreational instructional programs, such as the American Red Cross (ARC) adapted aquatic programs[1, 2] and the Young Men's Christian Association (YMCA) programs for the handicapped[3, 4] and traditional therapeutic hydrotherapy programs,[5-8] have been used in recreation and play programs as well as therapy for the disabled.

Aquatic programs which are properly designed and which integrate the recreational and therapeutic approaches can offer unique opportunities for initial learning as well as for reinforcing and practicing activities learned in other settings.[1] Objectives of one pool program are stated to be to "prepare the handicapped through aquatics to be contributing members of society."[9 (p. 431)] Daily living skills may be performed in the relevance of time and setting. The dual recreation and therapeutic benefits of water include: three dimensional exercise, perceptual stimulation, buoyancy and respiratory effects, psychological benefits, balance, and rotational control.[10] The motivational and therapeutic properties of water can provide a stimulating learning environment for even the most severely handicapped child. Developmental activities which are often impossible for the child on land can be accomplished in the water. These aquatic motor experiences often allow the disabled child temporary freedom from the usual confines of braces, wheelchairs and institutional cribs. Physical and emotional independence may also be improved, both short term during pool time, and over the long term after participation in a continuing aquatic program.[1,2,4] Games, fun, and the opportunity for success can easily be built into aquatic programs, which may be the disabled child's only form of recreation.

Several current situations exist in aquatic programs, however, which threaten the existence of integrated therapeutic and recreational approaches to aquatic programming and thus program effectiveness. These situations may be caused in part by the exclusive use of one approach, which fails to integrate the productive information and activities from the various program types to comprise a total approach.

## PROGRAM TYPES

Over the years, aquatic programs for disabled children have generally developed along several different lines. A thorough review of the literature and compiled survey data[11] supports the author's categorization of aquatic programs into three popular approaches: recreational, therapeutic and integrated.

### Recreational Programs

Programs labelled by the author as *recreational* are also *instructional* and are primarily conducted in recreational or community settings. Two national recreational aquatic programs for the disabled exist. The American Red Cross' adapted aquatic programs[1,2,12,13] and the YMCA's programs for the handicapped[3,4] are based upon the progressive swimming programs of each agency.[14,15] Recreational programs emphasize the development of play, having fun, and changing the behavior of the individual in a social environment. Further aims include improving swimming and water safety skills,[1-4,9,16] learning games,[1,2,16,17] increasing fitness and simply enjoying recreation.[9] Benefits and purposes for the recreational programs also involve general physiological, psychological, physical, social and educational aspects.

### Therapeutic Programs

Therapeutic programs are carried out under a physician's direction in physical therapy departments, or in other areas of the medical therapeutic setting. Physical therapists are usually the directors of therapeutic programs or the responsibility may be shared with other allied health professionals.

Therapeutic program staff use an approach which combines the neurophysiological treatment principles of hydrodynamics with underwater exercise techniques.[5,7,17] Emphasis here is on changing the pathology of the individual by using the water as a therapeutic medium. Applied treatment theory and methods are used in program design to meet treatment objectives for the individual child. The influence of the physical properties of water on the child's movement and position is also considered in designing individualized programs.[5,7,8,17] Specific objectives may include improving joint mobility, muscle strength, movement patterns and endurance. Activities tend to include anatomical movements which are often unrelated to each other, in contrast to the related swimming movements of game activities used in recreational programs.

As in other types of therapy, therapeutic aquatic programs are based upon indications for pool treatment relating to specific conditions which can benefit from the neurophysiological or physiological effects of the water.[5,7,8,17]

The benefits and rationales for therapeutic pool programs are several. Values include possible movement in all planes, development of stability, balance, and movement using buoyancy.[10, 17] Water facilitates gradation of exercise, relaxation and movement.[7, 18] Range of motion exercises, stretching, and spine mobility can be accomplished with decreased pain because of the hydrodynamic effects.[5,7]

### Integrated Programs

Aquatic programs which the author identifies as *integrated* are comprehensive programs in which both *recreational* and *therapeutic* aspects are combined in every possible element: goals, activities, staff composition and training, philosophy, and methods. Integrated programs combine the skills and fun of recreational programs with therapeutic treatment objectives, activities, and safety precautions. As an example, one integrated program's goals are: survival, exercise, and recreation.[19] Instructional and play activities to promote socialization, daily living skills, and the total welfare of the individual as well as restoration of maximal functions while developing a recreational outlet, are other stated goals.

Several principles are advocated in developing individualized integrated programs.[19] A thorough knowledge of the individual's medical, educational and emotional background is considered vital. Suitable conditions of learning including environmental conditions, session length, practice periods and progression of activities to meet an individual's needs are also important. Each individual is challenged to experience, explore, select, clarify and improve skills in activities and positive interpersonal relationships.

Integrated programs also consider the carryover of attitudes from the aquatic environment to the child's other functional settings to be of great importance. In describing the total aquatic program, one must consider the observations of other people involved with the child in other environments who notice and evaluate his performance and affect.[4] For example, improved parental attitude and acceptance of a child's asthma promoted greater opportunities, independence, and normalcy for the asthmatic child.[20] Subjective changes in the asthmatic child as a result of an aquatic program have also been documented.[21]

Integrated programs also focus on practicing and learning functional skills, both in and out of the water. Several integrated programs have developmental and learning objectives for the child.[10,18,20,22,23] Some integrated programs focus on academic, preacademic and sensorimotor learning,[22] while others focus on learning motor and daily living skills and broadening developmental experiences.[10,18,23] Reinforcement, transfer of learning, and integration of learned tasks across multiple tasks and environments as described in Gagne[24] and Tyler[25] are also encouraged in integrated programs.

## PROGRAMMATIC PROBLEMS AS POSSIBLE CONSEQUENCES OF THE RECREATIONAL/THERAPEUTIC DICHOTOMY

Traditionally the recreational/instructional aquatic programs and the therapeutic programs are exclusive of each other, resulting in a fragmentation of aquatic programming and very little integrated programming literature and practice. Because aquatic programs for the disabled tend to be unidisciplinary in orientation, the double benefits which the integrated aquatic approach offers are thereby forfeited. In addition, an increase in potential safety problems and a reduction in benefits that disabled children might receive through aquatic experiences appears to have resulted from the recreational/therapeutic dichotomy.

Analysis of the literature reveals discrepancies between these three aquatic approaches and program environments which can meet the multiple needs of the disabled child. The literature also contains clear evidence of other problems which appear, at least in part, to have been created by the polarization of the recreational and therapeutic approaches. The broadest problems appear to be the result of the exclusive philosophies of programs labeled either as recreational or as therapeutic. For example, the Red Cross programs[1,2] are considered therapeutic if they follow the recommendations of physicians or physical therapists. Another adaptive aquatic program for university students also exemplifies the dichotomy. Hutchens[26] notes that a program participant did not complete the program because of a "conflict with a physical therapy schedule."[(p. 45)] Instead of integrating the educational and treatment benefits of the aquatic program, swimming was forfeited for physical therapy.

The dichotomy between recreational and therapeutic programs is also exemplified in a survey of education needs by attitude discrepancies between recreational and therapeutic staffs. On the survey, physical therapists often indicated negative opinions about recreational programs. These therapists were negative primarily because of having observed safety problems or poor management of disabled children participating in some recreational programs. In addition, therapists often communicated common misconceptions about the type of direct benefits pool programs could offer the child. On the other hand, staff from recreational programs wanted their programs to remain strictly recreational in nature. Recreational staff did not view the therapeutic values of the physical therapy program (either for the pool or outside of the pool) as important in the survey. These polarized professional views on aquatic programs, expressed in the survey, demonstrated the strongest evidence of the rift between recreational and therapeutic staff.[11]

### Problems in Recreational Programs

The sometimes limited medical/therapeutic input in recreational programs can lead to problems of safety and communication. Safety problems may result if the recreational instructor's understanding of a child's abilities or disabling condition is inadequate. Sometimes training manuals include only brief information on disabilities and their relationship to aquatics.[4] Other times, the methods suggested for dealing with the disabilities are overly generalized in application without notation of necessary precautions. Inadequate mention is made in some recreational texts regarding the obligating influence that primitive reflexes may have on a child's movement or position.[1,4,16] Determination of optimal swimming position should be based on the individual's abilities and ease of breathing.[16] A position which facilitates breathing, however, may also stimulate a pathological or primitive reflex, as described by Barnes and coworkers,[27] Bobath and Bobath,[28] and Finnie;[29] this fact may not be mentioned.

The disabled child's other clinical symptoms are also sometimes inadequately defined in recreational program texts. Related problems in speech and breath control and the cough reflex problems which commonly affect children with cerebral palsy, are symptoms that may cause safety hazards if unanticipated by recreational instructors. The use of "natural" reflexes is advocated in some techniques.[19] Obligating reflexes,[27] however, which potentially interfere with the child's safety in the pool area are not addressed, nor are alternative ways of handling the child, as described by Finnie[29] to avoid those problems.

Another problem which appears to stem from a non-integrated knowledge base is a tendency toward inaccurate use of medical terminology and therapeutic principles. Misinterpretation, incomplete understanding, and faulty translation of the medical background information may also occur, resulting in incorrect usage and application of the methods. Examples include glossary definitions that are incorrectly adapted, incomplete, or taken out of context[19] and misleading pictures and descriptions of therapeutic principles such as body mechanics, injury prevention and efficient movement patterns.[1, 2, 19]

## Problems in Therapeutic Programs

Recent literature in therapeutic aquatic programs for the disabled is extremely limited. The scarce current therapeutic literature is primarily authored by Canadian or British physicians or physical therapists.[10,17,30,31] American authors have written the classical therapeutic literature. Aquatics appears to have a more widespread use in Great Britain than in the United States, both historically and presently, perhaps resulting from an apparently heavier emphasis in professional training which two British-trained physical therapists identified.[32,33]

Other problems identified in therapeutic literature seem to reflect the unidisciplinary background of therapists in pool programs, including polarized perspectives, criticism of recreational approaches, limited application, and the economics of pool programs. Unlike recreational staff, physical therapists are not usually encouraged to incorporate techniques other than their own therapeutic techniques into programs. Few learning-transfer activities between the therapeutic pool and the child's other programs seem to occur. Therapeutic program staff too often fail to consider recreational or integrated program characteristics. For example, Duffield[17] recommends therapeutic techniques only with "lower motor neuron diseases or patients with painful joint problems with weakness and decreased range of motion and no neurological deficits.[(p.50)] Patients with upper motor neuron lesions (i.e., with spasticity, occurring in many children with cerebral palsy) should instead receive swimming instruction as "pool therapy has not been found to be of value."[(p.50)] Duffield's statements imply an "all swimming" or "all therapy" approach.

Although the use of hydrodynamics for gradation of exercise (hydrotherapy) is primarily a therapeutic technique, the discussion of the effects of physical properties of water on position and movement are usually not exhaustive with the exception of Duffield.[17]

Duffield[17] and Harris[18] advocate the use of the pool for development of balance, movement, and motor control, but Duffield[17] states that an ataxic individual derives little therapeutic benefit from pool programs because of increased balance problems resulting from the water's turbulence. This rationale, however, seems incongruous with general treatment practice, as therapeutic intervention generally begins just at the point where a child has difficulty in accomplishing an activity.

According to some authors, aquatics is not widely used in therapeutic programs because of cost, lack of need, and hazards to health. Duffield[17] discusses the cost of obtaining and maintaining a pool, the time and manpower required for individual treatment sessions, and the transportation problems all as negative aspects of pool programming. Although generally believing that pool therapy is a valuable technique, she warns that "too many pool sessions can psychologically make the patient too dependent on the pool when the aim of a good medical management is independence of pools, machines, doctors, and therapists."(p. 72) In this statement Duffield[17] implies a dichotomy between aquatic and medical management. In discussing equipment for physical therapy in residential facilities for developmentally delayed children, Williams[34] states that "a program with developmental emphasis for infants and young children will probably have limited need for hydrotherapy."(p. 457) Several programs for the developmentally disabled, however, may be found in the literature.[3,22,23,31]

Kolb[5] notes the problem of the need for both a therapist and an aide in the pool, as well as scheduling difficulties because of necessary dressing time before and after the actual pool sessions. Danger of spread of infection, fatigue of the therapist and patient, and respiratory infections are other disadvantages to pool programs stated in therapeutic literature. Solutions to these problems identified in therapeutic programs are in the integrated aquatic approaches discussed later in this paper.

## Problems in Integrated Programs

The most apparent problems found in both the literature and practice are first, the scarcity of integrated programs and second that integrated programs usually tend to originate from and reflect either the therapeutic or the recreational approach. Because the staff, the methods, and the professional training are not thoroughly integrated, many so-called integrated programs also have the programmatic problems of the recreational or of the therapeutic approaches. Otherwise, integrated programs more closely than any other approach, approximate the type of program which can best meet the needs of the disabled child. Many fewer problems appear to exist in integrated programs than in either recreational or therapeutic programs. In addition, solutions to the problems identified in either recreational or therapeutic programs may usually be found in either the alternate approach or in the integrated approach.

Recreational programs have need of therapeutic input regarding the functional and adaptive implications of various disabilities, safety precautions, medical or therapeutic terms, and application of the principles of hydrotherapy. These needs usually can be met either by direct service contributions from therapeutic program staff, or by therapeutic input integrated into on-going recreational programs. The addition of therapeutic program staff to already-established recreational programs could thus promote the use of aquatics as a therapeutic adjunct. Cost problems of pool facilities and of maintenance[17] may be absorbed by soliciting donations or by requesting federal funding for PL 94-142 or rental of a community YMCA, ARC, motel, or private pool.[1,2,4] Initiation of new programs or integration into on-going programs at these facilities are both possible options. The need for treatment of one patient at a time or for both a therapist and an aide[5] may be decreased or eliminated with an interdisciplinary or trans-disciplinary team approach as with Mason's program.[31] Group pool activities for children and the use of closely supervised, trained volunteers, parents, and community personnel reduce the need for one adult (or therapist) per child (Kolb's[5] criticism), as well as encourages socialization.[1,2] Duffield's[17] warning against becoming dependent on pools disregards the social, psychological, and recreational benefits that pool programs provide. Daily permission from medical personnel for individuals who are scheduled to swim reduces the potential danger of spreading infection. Fatigue from exposure to warm water can be reduced through close supervision, or by altering the length of time spent on the activity or in the water.

## *PROGRAM PERSONNEL: THEIR ROLES & TRAINING*

Staff composition and the functions these professionals perform appear to vary to a small degree according to the type of program in which they serve, and to a large degree as a result of staff training. Variations in program types again seem to be responsible for many of these staff differences.

Professional functioning in the aquatic program environment often requires assumption of roles expanded beyond that of clinician, for example, to the role of educator, advocate, or consultant. As training emphasis is on the clinician role, other roles are often more difficult to assume. Filling new roles in a setting other than the primary setting in which the professional functions (often the case in aquatic programs), is even more difficult. Many professionals do not have the knowledge base or experience needed for adaptation to the new setting or the new role. Differences in role expectations may conflict with those of other people already established in the setting, or for whom the setting is primary. Findings of the survey of educational needs of physical therapists, community pool personnel, and other allied health professionals working with the developmentally delayed[11] revealed discrepancies between role expectations and actual capabilities. The survey indicated that community aquatic program staff had professional role expectations of therapists as educators, consultants, and resource people. Community personnel stated a reliance on medical professionals for program support, patient referrals, and medical advice. Community personnel asked professionals to provide consultation related to rationales for pool use and integration of individual goals. The therapeutic professionals were also asked to provide skill adaptations and to incorporate prescribed movements into the pool programs for individual children.

The therapists, however, were unable to meet those needs because of the lack of interest, knowledge or skills in aquatic programs. The survey[11] results indicated that physical therapists did not have the practical knowledge and skills necessary to design and implement aquatic programs to meet those role expectations of the community program staff. Noted on the survey were deficiencies in:

1. knowledge of evaluation techniques for individual children in aquatic programs;
2. ability to incorporate treatment goals and methods into pool programs;
3. knowledge of treatment progression methods;
4. integration and transfer of transdisciplinary program activities, goals, and methods from the pool to the traditional program environment;
5. knowledge of contraindications, methods and neurophysiological rationales for pool use for specific disability groups;
6. knowledge of pool facility and community program availability (if the therapist did not have a pool within the facility of employment, the therapist seemed unaware of alternatives); and
7. knowledge of existing possibilities for using other pools or for having associations with ongoing community pool programs.

### Recreational Program Staff

Recreational program staff include adapted aquatic instructors[1,2] for the handicapped,[3,4] instructor-trainers,[13] aides,[12] volunteers (teachers, allied health personnel, parents and disabled persons).[1,2,12,35] Both the YMCA[3,4] and ARC[1,2] encourage persons to serve as consultants, to promote rapport, and to serve as role models. Both ARC and YMCA programs also emphasize team education and cooperation for an individualized approach to the child's needs and encourage therapists and school personnel to join their children in swimming.

Efficiently functioning aquatic programs require assumption of multiple roles, as emphasized by YMCA program training.[4] Administrative tasks of scheduling and pool selection are deemed important. Other functions necessary for efficient aquatic programs include: public relations, documentation and recording, medical and safety considerations, and education of the public, parents and staff.

Aides and volunteers may assist in the locker room and do other non-swimming tasks such as transportation, record-keeping, and on-deck spotting as well as teach under the direction of an instructor.[3]

The professional training of recreational program staff is in recreation, physical education, or progressive swimming with further training and certification in the characteristics of disabilities and techniques for adapting skills and activities for the disabled.

Instructor education for ARC[1,2,13] and YMCA[3,4] programs involves theory and supervised practical experience with disabled individuals, both in and out of the pool. Instructor training seminars include basic information, such as the roles of program staff, a synopsis of the various disabilities, and the effect of the impairment in aquatics, along with related aquatic safety and functional management techniques. Body mechanics, transfer techniques, and management of assistive devices and other equipment, water safety and swimming skills methods are included in practical and discussion sessions for the instructor candidates. Both general and specific methods are described for working with persons having various disabilities on safety skills, strokes, pool transfers, and locker room requirements. Additional objectives of the training institutes include identification and differentiation of disciplinary concerns and treatment approaches, as well as building and using of team resources in an aquatic transdisciplinary framework.[3,4]

## Therapeutic Program Staff

Physical therapists, physical therapy aides, and physical therapy assistants usually comprise the therapeutic program staff. Other allied health professions sometimes direct but more often are involved to a lesser degree in therapeutic programs, under the direction of a physical therapist. Therapeutic program staff apply principles in performing underwater exercises as an adjunct to other therapeutic means of accomplishing therapeutic goals for the individual.

As background for therapeutic aquatic programs, physical therapists receive training in the neurophysiology of normal and dysfunctional development, anatomy, and neurophysiology.[36] Curricula also include treatment theory and the problem-solving approach to the selection of indicated modalities, as well as identification of contraindications and precautions for treatment. The focus is on independence and safety during treatment and throughout all aspects of life, including vital and daily living skills.[35] As specific background for therapeutic aquatic programs, training in hydrotherapy involves the application of the physical effects of water in order to derive the following objectives:

1. physiological and diagnosis-specific indications for treatment; and
2. a method of gradation of exercise, primarily focusing on anatomical movements.[35]

### Integrated Program Staff

The composition and training of staff for integrated programs is combined. Personnel for integrated programs involve a team combination of recreational program staff and therapeutic program staff, all working to plan and implement the aquatic program. Role expectations and an expressed importance of medical support in recreational programs which could represent integrated staffing patterns are stated as: "inclusion of physicians and paramedical specialists provide parents and the community assurance that the pool activities are being conducted safely."[4(p.14)] Red Cross-sponsored adapted aquatic programs encourage cooperation and input from paramedical staff for "technically accurate, well-researched, current, and authoritative information."[2 (p.130)]

Medical advisors, either allied health professionals or physicians, are recommended as part of the aquatic team to provide direct medical and therapeutic assistance in advisory capacities and as instructor training faculty.[1,2] The 1976 Dulcy survey, however, seemed to indicate that these health professionals often did not have the necessary skills, and that their attitude differences prevented their joining the aquatic team.[11]

Training of staff for integrated programs theoretically would involve both recreational methods[1-4] and therapeutic methods, the latter in greater depth and detail than only recommended therapeutic input. Integrated staff training would also include the basic therapeutic management, positioning and facilitation, and developmental techniques such as Banus[37] recommends for all pediatric professionals. Integrated program staff training would be conducted by an integrated faculty and would focus on teaching functional skills both in and out of the pool.[18,23] It would encourage reinforcement, transfer of learning, and integration of learned skills across multiple environments, tasks and settings.[22,23]

The differences in training and roles and the resulting gaps between the two major approaches and a comprehensive approach seem somewhat apparent in the immediately preceding discussion and also seem to illustrate the need for an integrated approach.

### Professional Staff and Training Problems

Current literature supports the previous survey[11] and further identifies professional factors which interfere with optimal pool programming for the disabled child. The survey identified educational needs in the area of aquatic programming and additionally pinpointed some problems in aquatic programs for the disabled. The discrepancies identified in the survey (six years ago) between present conditions and those conditions desired still appear to exist in current programs. The following professional problems in pool programming were identified in the survey:

1. inadequate professional skills to meet the needs of the individual disabled child or to design activities for transfer and reinforcement of learning;
2. inadequate provision of safety precautions;
3. ineffective communication, especially between professionals who serve disabled persons in various settings;
4. inability of both individual professionals and of teams to integrate other commonly used models of professional service delivery within the aquatic environment;
5. lack of a theoretical frame of reference for aquatic programs;
6. lack of awareness of available program resources;
7. inability to provide rationales for using aquatics;
8. insufficient documentation of data, research or training materials for aquatics for the disabled; and
9. lack of integration of recreational and therapeutic professional staff composition, professional training, and competencies.[11]

## PROGRAM METHODS: CONTRIBUTIONS TO THE INTEGRATED APPROACH

Although most methods are traditionally attributed to either recreational or therapeutic programs, these methods may be viewed as having dual (integrated) purposes to meet the individual's integrated needs and program goals. An important aspect of integrated techniques is the emphasis on carryover of activities between the aquatic program environment and other learning and treatment environments, such as building "swimming readiness" in the classroom by learning about pools and water, and in perceptual and motor developmental activities in the gym. This type of program considers the child's total development and learning process in a total program approach rather than as isolated developmental tasks.

### Recreationally-Oriented Methods

Methods originating primarily from recreational programs include: water adjustment, safety skills, swimming, academic reinforcement, movement exploration, and aquatic games.

Swimming and water safety skills, more widely used in recreational programs, are incorporated as appropriate to the child's needs and adapted to the individual's abilities so he may accomplish them.[1-5,9,10,17,30] Swimming progressions are preceded with preswimming[10,18,22] and water adjustment skills.[1,2,7,10,17,31] Preliminary skills of standing, walking and jumping in all directions in the water prior to swimming are recommended by Reid.[10] Based on learning theory,[25,38] water adjustment skills enable the individual to learn about the new water environment and to make the necessary physical and emotional adjustments as essential preparation to learning any further aquatic activities. Water adjustment activities should be fun, build confidence, and progress at the child's rate.[18] Water adjustment also involves finding, maintaining, and practicing a body position[1,2,17] which relates to kinesthetic and vestibular perception, motor learning, and development of control of both movement and position. Based upon the author's categorization, water adjustment methods include aspects of an integrated approach.

Although swimming is primarily a recreational technique, swimming skills are included in instructional curricula as well as strongly therapeutic curricula. Teaching a method of propulsion early in the program is considered important for motivational purposes.[31] Propulsion provides satisfaction in accomplishment since swimming proficiency is usually not possible with the multiply-handicapped child.[31] The learning sequence progression for teaching propulsion is first learning isolated underwater arm movements, then the leg movements, and finally combining the movements.[1,2,7,17,39] A specific relief stroke related to the medical conditions and safety needs of people with specific disabilities may also be taught.[5]

Recreational aquatic programs emphasize the child's safety at all times in the water, in the locker rooms, and in the entire program ecosystem. The goal of personal water safety is reached through five well-established methods of basic aquatic safety skills.[1,2,4,5,7,30] Red Cross programs advocate that a part of each pool session should be spent working on safety skills with each child and, however minimally, learning these five safety skills to the maximum of his or her ability. Of the water safety skills, several programs emphasize breath control or include breath control as a major component.[1,2,18,31,40] The Five Basic Safety Skills[1,2] are:

1. breath control;
2. back float and recovery (to a position in which the individual may regain a safe breathing position, most frequently to a standing position);
3. prone float and recovery;
4. turning over from back to front and front to back floating positions; and
5. changing directions. Note that these skills are also developmental skills.

A natural integrated relationship exists between some land and water activities. The land gross motor developmental activities of rolling and standing are equivalent to "rolling over" and "recovery" from the floating position in aquatic programs, and the therapeutic breathing exercises are the same as the breath control skills of the aquatic basic safety skills.[1,2] Safety skills can be used as an activity for transfer of motor control and learning between treatment and aquatic settings.

Movement exploration, a recreational technique originating from physical education, may be used both in and out of the pool and involves the child in a series of problem-solving experiences.[1-4,16,30,41] The objectives of movement exploration activities are to learn to understand, control and improve body movement. The individual's responses to the problems take the form of practical application of kinesis, body scheme, and perceptual relationships. Through these responses, the individual promotes self-understanding and body awareness. In this way, sensory input and kinesthetic feedback are integrated with the mechanism of motor control. Success is assured as the child is challenged to solve motor problems within his or her own movement repertory and capability. Psychological as well as perceptual motor development may, therefore, be facilitated through movement exploration.

Academic reinforcement techniques emphasize teaching for transfer from one environment to the other because similar activities, principles, techniques, and equipment are often used in the pool, classroom, gym and aquatic program.[1-3,16,22] Aquatic games may incorporate perceptual and language concepts the child is working on both in the classroom and in the pool.

The game approach[1-3,16,22] is commonly used with children especially in recreational programs but is also presented in an integrated manner with stated therapeutic purposes.[17,31] Games tend to involve the child more completely in the activity than other techniques, by shifting the focus away from the individual, increasing interest and participation and decreasing pressure to perform. Games also tend to raise the individual's frustration tolerance, to stimulate curiosity, improve creativity and motivate the desire to learn in the water. Individualized games often incorporate swimming, fundamental movement, perceptual motor, and academic skills in order to enhance the transfer of learning from one environment to the other.[16]

### Therapeutically-Oriented Methods

Methods used primarily in therapeutic programs include anatomical movements often used in underwater exercise, progressive exercises through the use of hydrodynamics, developmental sequencing of activities, and other specific treatment methods. The individual's clinical symptoms are used to determine specific safety techniques as well as methods to develop the greatest independence in activities of daily living.

Therapeutic program authors outline methods for the progression of exercise in aquatics.[5,7,8,17] Hydrodynamic properties of the water, which influence the individual's position and movement in the water, are the basis of exercise progression. Exercise progression involves the use of buoyancy, first as assistance, then as support, and finally as resistance to active movement. Various developmental positions used to enhance movement and function are also presented[17,18,29,30] and are modified for the individual according to the amount or location of support and the emphasis of anatomical movement relative to the position in the water.[5,7] Kolb[5] and Harris[18] advocate relaxation activities as an essential part of pool programs for all patients. Rehabilitative methods for improving safety and independence in activities of daily living and pool entry and exit are also important parts of pool programs.[1,2,17,31] Transfers, toileting, showering and other skills may be learned and practiced appropriately and quickly because of the added motivation of going into the pool.

## DISCUSSION

The recreational therapeutic dichotomy in aquatic programming for disabled children has created breakdowns in the entire system.

The input to the system consists of recreational and therapeutic programs, each with their unidisciplinary philosophies, goals and methods. The composition of the staff and their teaching and related problems have been discussed. Consideration of the disabled child, his needs and abilities, is filtered only through one approach or the other, rather than in a comprehensive manner.

A vicious cycle of problems exists (Figure 2). Insufficient medical therapeutic input either in training or consultation to recreational programs may lead to a lack of or deficient knowledge about safety considerations, developmental needs, diagnosis and functional abilities of the child. Safety problems may result in programs having poor reputations. Therapists tend to mistrust recreational programs and this causes a further decrease in input, decrease in efficiency and further safety problems.

Aquatic programming processes include: developmental, communication, aquatic, medical/therapeutic and educational—both of staff and of the child. Developmental aquatic programming is sparse and poorly integrated with other types of programs. All methods of communication—written, verbal and non-verbal—perpetuate the problems from the unidisciplinary approach from which they originate. Cross lines of communication and input often do not occur. Documentation and research are limited. Education also continues along the orientation of initial input. Medical/therapeutic service intervention occurs often in a vacuum—with poor input or output to any other area except perhaps other medical therapeutic settings and professionals. Aquatic programming processes or the methods used by aquatic program staff, are also split from input to output.

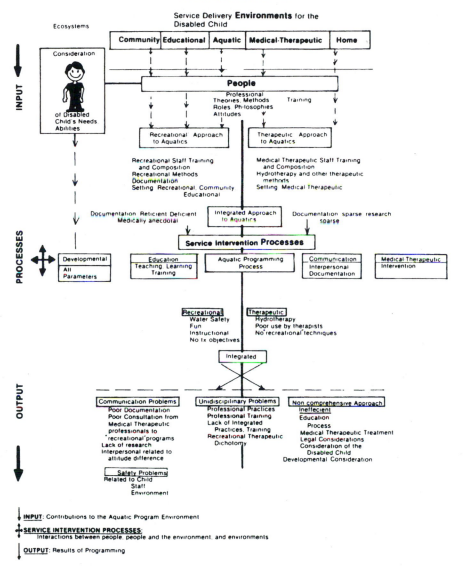

**Figure 1**

**A SYSTEM ANALYSIS OF PROBLEMS IN AQUATIC PROGRAMS FOR DISABLED CHILDREN**

The results of programming, or outcomes, are reflective of the earlier problems. Pools remain empty because staff either doesn't know how to design and progress individualized pool programs, or because of knowledge of the projected costs of the program without knowledge of

**Figure 2:    Vicious Cycle of Problems
in Aquatic Programs**

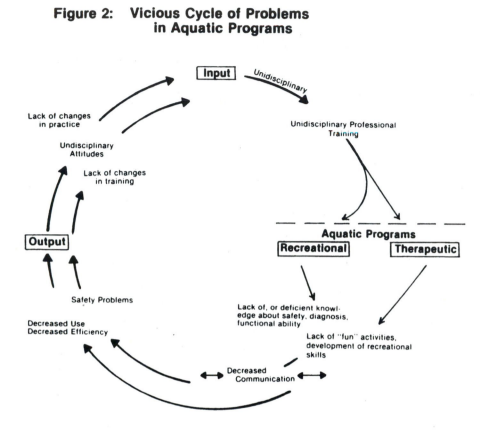

the benefits. Unidisciplinary programs and professional training continue to flourish. Attitude differences exist, further hampering communication and chances for cooperative programs. Documentation of program method and approaches (integrated especially) is sparse. Research articles are rare. Safety problems exist in areas of the individual child's needs, lack of environmental considerations, and staff skills and knowledge. Inefficiency exists in developmental and medical/therapeutic treatment and carryover between pool and other treatment and educational environments. Consideration of legalities often is not given.

## CONCLUSIONS

The goals, methods and philosophies of aquatic programs for the disabled children, as well as staff composition and training tend to persist in their recreational or therapeutic orientations. The combination, or integration of these components may be used to create an optimal program by structuring them in an integrated program to comprehensively meet the unique needs of a child. Once identified, the gaps between current and desired programs, frequently as a consequence of the recreational/ therapeutic dichotomy, seem to indicate that a new model is needed to encompass and integrate all the vital aspects of programming.

These problems, or discrepancies from the ideal, and an idealized program, were used as a rationale in developing a transdisciplinary model framework and guidelines.

## REFERENCES

1. American Red Cross: *Swimming for Persons with Physical and Mental Impairments.* Washington DC, 1977.

2. American Red Cross: *Methods in Adapted Aquatics: A Manual for the Instructor.* Washington DC, 1977.

3. American Association of Health, Physical Education and Recreation: *A Practical Guide for Teaching the Mentally Retarded to Swim.* Washington DC, Young Men's Christian Association, 1969.

4. Reynolds G (ed): *A Swimming Program for the Handicapped.* New York, National YMCA, 1973.

5. Kolb ME: Principles of underwater exercise. *Phys Ther Rev* 37:1336-1365, 1957.

6. Lowman, CL: Therapeutic indications for pool therapy. *Phys Ther Rev* 37:224, 1957.

7. Lowman CL, Roen SG: *Therapeutic Use of Pools and Tanks.* Philadelphia, WB Saunders, 1952.

8. Moor FB, Peterson SC, Manwell EM, et al.: *Manual of Hydrotherapy and Massage.* Mountainview CA, Pacific Press Publishing Association, 1964.

9. Muhl WT: Aquatics for the Handicapped. *J Health Phys Educ and Recreat* Feb:42-43, 1976.

10. Reid MJ: Activities in water based on the halliwick method. *Child Care Health Dev* 1(4):217-233, 1975.

11. Dulcy FH: Survey of educational needs of personnel working in aquatics for the handicapped. Park Forest South, IL, 1976.

12. American Red Cross: *Swimming for the Handicapped: A Manual for the Aide.* Washington DC, 1974.

13. American Red Cross: *Guide for Training Instructors in Adapted Aquatics Programs.* Washington DC, 1977.

14. American Red Cross: *Swimming and Water Safety Textbook.* Washington DC, 1968.

15. Arnold LC, Freeman RW: *Progressive Swimming and Springboard Diving Program.* New York, National YMCA, 1972.

16. Georgia Dept. of Human Resources, Division of Mental Health and Retardation: *Aquatic Games and Swimming Techniques for the Handicapped.* Atlanta, 1976.

17. Duffield MH (ed): *Exercise in Water.* New York, McMillan and Co., 1976.

18. Harris, SR: Neurodevelopmental treatment approach for teaching swimming to cerebral palsied children. *Phys Ther* 58:979-983, 1978.

19. Newman J: *Swimming for Children with Physical and Sensory Impairments.* Springfield, IL, Charles C. Thomas, 1976.

20. Fitch K, Morton AR, Blansky BA: Effects of swimming training on children with asthma. *Arch Dis Child* 51:190-194, 1976.

21. Chai H, Falliers CJ: Controlled swimming in asthmatic children: An evaluation of physiological and subjective data. *J Allergy* (abs) 41(2):93, 1968.

22. Lawrence CC, Hackett LC: *Water Learning.* Palo Alto, CA, Peek Publications, 1975.

23. Burnell B: *Swimming Pool Program.* Park Forest South, IL, Elisabeth Ludeman Developmental Center, 1976.

24. Gagne RM: *Essentials of Learning for Instruction.* Hinsdale, IL, Drydan Press, 1974.

25. Tyler R: *Basic Principles of Curriculum and Instruction.* Chicago, The University of Chicago Press, 1949.

26. Hutchens GL: An action adapted program. *J Health, Phys Educ and Recreat* May:42-45, 1974.

27. Barnes MC, Crutchfield CA, Heriza CB: *The Neurophysiological Basis of Patient Treatment (Vol. II): Reflexes and Motor Development.* Morgantown, WV, Stokesville Publishing Co., 1978.

28. Bobath K, Bobath B: The neurodevelopmental approach to treatment. In Pearson PH, Williams CE: *Physical Therapy Services in the Developmental Disabilities.* Springfield, IL, Charles C. Thomas, 1972, pp. 114-186.

29. Finnie NR: *Handling the Young Cerebral Palsied Child at Home* (2nd ed). New York, EP Hutton Co., 1975.

30. Elkington HJ: The effective use of the pool. *Physiotherapy* 57:452-460, 1971.

31. Mason C: Pool activities with the multiply handicapped child. *Nursing Mirror* 25:50-52, 1975.

32. Yucel N: Personal communication regarding British physical therapy training. Atlanta, 1979.

33. Brown B: Personal communication regarding British physical therapy training. Chicago, 1975.

34. Williams CE: Physical therapy in residential facilities. In Pearson PH, Williams CE (eds), *Physical Therapy Services in the Developmental Disabilities.* Springfield, IL, Charles C. Thomas, 1972.

35. Georgia Chapter, American Physical Therapy Association: Standards of Practice. Atlanta, 1975.

36. American Physical Therapy Association: Competencies in Physical Therapy: An Analysis of Practice, San Diego, Courseware Inc., 1977.

37. Banus BS: *The Developmental Therapist.* Thorofare, NJ, Chas C Slack Inc, 1972.

38. Robb, MD: *The Dynamics of Skill Acquisition.* Englewood Cliffs, NJ, Prentice-Hall, Inc., 1972.

39. Stewart JB: Exercises in water. In Licht, S (ed): *Therapeutic Exercise* (2nd ed). Baltimore, Waverly Press, Inc., 285-296, 1965.

40. Adams MA, Chandler, LS: Effects of a physical therapy program on vital capacity of patients with muscular dystrophy. *Phys Ther* 54:494-496, 1974.

41. Moran J, Kalakian LH: *Movement Experiences for the Mentally Retarded or Emotionally Disturbed Child.* Minneapolis, Burgess Publishing Company, 1974.

# A Theoretical Aquatic Service Intervention Model for Disabled Children

Faye H. Dulcy, MMSc, RPT

**ABSTRACT.** Existing problems in aquatic programs for disabled children seemed to indicate the need for an idealized program model. As a solution strategy, a developmental, transdisciplinary theoretical model and accompanying guidelines were developed. A panel of experts representing various disciplines in aquatics validated both through use of the Delphi technique. The foundation of the validated Aquatic Service Intervention Model for Disabled Children consists of theories, traditional service delivery models, and ecological elements. Derived from this foundation are considerations of environments; professions or disciplines; developmental, communication, medical-therapeutic, educational, and aquatic programming processes; and safety and legal constraints.

The writer concludes that an integrated, transcisciplinary aquatic program can bridge the gap between recreational and therapeutic programming approaches. A high degree of consensus by the panelists indicates that professionals can better approximate the ideal attitudes, goals, training, and functions in this type of framework, than in traditional programs where a chasm seems to exist, and unidisciplinary practices prevail.

## INTRODUCTION: MODEL EMPHASES AND RATIONALES

Problems described in the previous article, existing in the literature and practice, spurred the development of a theoretical model which integrates recreational and therapeutic approaches to aquatic programming for disabled children. The purpose of this article is to describe the Guidelines and theoretical Aquatic Service Intervention Model for Disabled Children (ASIMDC) which a multidisciplinary panel of experts have validated.

## CONSTRUCTS OF THE MODEL

### Ecological Construct

Analysis of the constituents of both an aquatic program and of other service intervention models for disabled children indicated that the environment, the people, and the services or methods provided by the people are vital elements of consideration in aquatic service intervention. In ecological theory, these three elements of *environments, people,* and *pro-*

*cesses* comprise an ecosystem which is a theoretical unit and an interactional system of living with the nonliving habitat.[1] The processes are defined as the interactions which occur between people, people and the environment, and between environments.[1]

Other service delivery models used in the disabled child's learning and treatment environments are potentially applicable to the aquatic program environment. The processes of development, communication, teaching and learning, and treatment are common to all service intervention environments. The aquatic program may also be related to professional health care and educational models, which are based upon established theories of development, special education, and medical-therapeutic service delivery.

### Integrated Developmental Therapy Construct

Children continuously learn and develop, therefore, intervention experiences should be provided consistently and continuously to the disabled child.[2-5] Optimal functioning may be facilitated in the environment which is natural to the child.[4] An integrated model of intervention allows the child to develop needed skills continuously in a natural environment, rather than only during the relatively short training sessions of an isolated intervention or therapy model. Skills that are taught and practiced in many settings, as in an integrated intervention model, have the best opportunity to generalize to the other settings.

In this way, all personnel in the child's environment become facilitators of the child's developmental and learning processes by promoting the same goals and activities.[3] People in developmental, educational, medical-therapeutic and home settings thus comprise the developmental team whose members apply principles to facilitate, strengthen, and generalize desirable responses, and ensure continuous attention to safety and optimal function. Based on these premises, the aquatic programming environment is a logical and needed addition to the traditional learning and therapy environments in an integrated model of service intervention.

As comprehensive intervention is ideally integrated into all aspects of the child's life, services are most effectively provided not only directly to the child, but also indirectly through consultation, education or advisement from other people in the child's environment.[2-4,6] In this way, integration and carryover of services may be maximized so that a few trained professionals may effectively serve the disabled child's needs.

### Integrated Recreational and Therapeutic Aquatic Approach Construct

The panelists validated the concept of an integrated recreational and therapeutic aquatic approach as the normative approach. Although individual Guidelines related only to the pure recreational or therapeutic approaches to aquatics, both approaches, rather than one or the other approach, were approved. Responses show that simultaneously using both approaches (or the integrated approach, as defined by the author), reflected the ideal program.

## Coordinated, Transdisciplinary Services Construct

In order for the ASIMDC to be a comparable and supplemental educational treatment medium, the input, transfer, and integration relationships between the other traditional service intervention models and the aquatic ecosystem were emphasized. The most effective model of service intervention for disabled children includes coordinated services of professionals in many disciplines who integrate services into all aspects of the child's life.[2,4,6] Effective service delivery models involve personnel working as a team, with each professional assuming multiple roles of service delivery expanded beyond that of clinician.[1,3,6,7]

Professionals practice at various disciplinary levels of complexity, ranging from unidisciplinary (involving only one's own discipline) to transdisciplinary practices. In the transdisciplinary approach, the most complex model of service delivery, the team members are committed to the teaching/learning process and to provision of services across traditional role boundaries.[8] In this way, each specialist becomes a technologist in his developmental specialty, but is a technician in applying the methods of the other specialty areas.[7] In the transdisciplinary team approach, the professionals' disciplinary boundaries are bridged[8] as when professionals with a broad theoretical basis of developmental theory apply developmental techniques from all traditional disciplines to their own treatment.[2]

Combining ecological theory[1] with the transdisciplinary approach to service delivery in the ASIMDC is a logical progression. Each ecological element (people, service intervention processes, and environments) is an important consideration in models of service delivery for the disabled child as well as in the transdisciplinary approach. Transfer and integration of the traditional service delivery models to an aquatic program model, because of the various professional roles and necessary intervention processes, would thus bring about a transdisciplinary aquatic approach.

The majority of existing programs and the training and literature related to aquatic programs for handicapped children are unidisciplinary, intradisciplinary, or multidisciplinary apparently contributing to the perpetuation of the recreational therapeutic dichotomy. Few programs are interdisciplinary,[9] and even fewer are even partially transdisciplinary.[10] The transdisciplinary approach, which is integrated, assures the most comprehensive program possible.

### Transfer, Integration and Carryover of Aquatic Activities Construct

The transfer, integration, and carryover of activities into and out of the aquatic environment are among the most important constructs (as an application of learning theory[11-13] in the ASIMDC. The model, in this case, applies learning theory to both the professional and his learning and functioning (in the Professional/Disciplinary Component, Level IV, B) and to the child's learning. For example, each child should have the opportunity to practice and generalize activities of daily living in a variety of environments. Professionals, likewise, should apply their professional learning and expertise from traditional service intervention environments to the aquatic environment, as well as perform their same professional functions.

### Educational Program and Legal Constructs

Application of the ASIMDC to aquatic programs as part of the child's educational program was a strong emphasis in the development of the model. The following factors supported and created this emphasis:

1. Specific mention of aquatic programs in Public Law 94-142;[14, 15] and
2. Increase in the number of aquatic programs included as part of the disabled child's educational curricular or extracurricular activities.

Another important objective in developing the ASIMDC and Guidelines was compliance with regulations cited in Federal legislation. Part of the intent of the study[16] was to develop an aquatic model which may be used as an alternative supplemental educational medium for the provision of services related to Public Law 94-142.[14] The target population for the model, therefore, was disabled children in the age range served by Bureau of Education for the Handicapped. Because of the developmental and treatment nature of the aquatic model, however, application to older developmentally delayed individuals is equally appropriate.

Some unusual parts of the ASIMDC Guidelines are legal considerations as applied to professional practice and those which are setting-related. One main reason for including the Legal Constraints as labeled in the ASIMDC and Guidelines is that little is written about the liabilities or responsibilities of various professionals who practice in the aquatic environment. Both the Dulcy survey[17] and the literature imply that if medical professionals were involved in the aquatic program process, much of the liability or responsibility would be transferred from the recreational personnel to the medical-therapeutic professionals. Indeed, the ramifications of professional responsibilities are probably not well known to either recreational or therapeutic staff members. Legal guidelines were also deemed important in order to apply the laws which define practices within a particular setting; for example, laws define the educational setting which must be provided for handicapped children.

## METHODS OF MODEL AND GUIDELINE DEVELOPMENT AND VALIDATION

The study[16] involved three parts. First, a five level ecological model framework for an integrated, transdisciplinary aquatic service delivery model was developed using the systems approach. Next, guidelines reflecting each ASIMDC level were proposed and written in form of a Delphi questionnaire. Finally validation of the Guidelines, and therefore of the ASIMDC framework, was obtained by evaluation of the Delphi questionnaire from a panel of experts in various fields associated with aquatics.

The ASIMDC was viewed as a system whose parts function both together and independently to achieve required results.[18] A system analysis of the problems in aquatics and identification of the requirements of the aquatic program ecosystem that would, if satisfied, meet the identified needs, provided the system approach framework used in model development.

The initial step in the systems approach is to set an ideal. The ASIMDC was developed to incorporate the characteristics of a variety of types of theoretical models including, most importantly, service delivery models and normative systems. The normative system is the most effective and efficient way to cause a transition from a less favorable to a more favorable system state,[19 (p. 464)] and may be said to approximate the ideal.

The normative ASIMDC was idealized by the author to have the following characteristics:

1. consideration of the total needs of the disabled child;
2. integration of recreational and therapeutic aquatic approaches;
3. transdisciplinary aquatic training and practices;
4. child, personnel, and environmental safety; and
5. efficient service delivery in each of the following areas:
   a. developmental intervention for the child,
   b. medical therapeutic treatment,
   c. educational processes applied to both the involved professionals and to the disabled child,
   d. communication and documentation,
   e. legalities relating to the practice of specific disciplines and to the provision of services for the disabled child within specific environments, and
   f. consideration of the nature of environmental benefits and dangers.

Secondly, the author analyzed the results of a survey of educational needs[17] in order to identify problems in individual areas, problems in the functioning of the entire system, and problems in the interrelationships of the parts of the system which interfere with the realization of the ideal.

The third step involved delineation of characteristics which are unique either to the current state or to the desired system.[18, 20] These characteristics were identified through the educational needs survey,[17] the review of the literature,[16] and examination and comparison of current aquatic programs with other traditional service intervention models for the disabled child.[16] These traditional service intervention models served as the archetypes, or original patterns, for the derived ASIMDC. The service delivery models, or service intervention models, are comprised of the professionals who provide services and the various roles, methods, and theories which the professionals use as part of the service intervention processes. These traditional models include: medical therapeutic, educational, home and, to some degree, aquatic.

Fourth, the author defined and categorized the problem areas (or gaps between the current and desired system state) in the simplest, most mutually exclusive form.[19, 20] The problems associated with each area were approached, both as separate entities and in relation to the other parts and to the whole.[18, 20] For example, the developmental level of a child is considered both as part of the developmental process and as a safety consideration. In this way, the Guidelines are meant to influence changes in several interrelated areas and, in turn, to narrow the gap between what now exists and the ideal. Using an ecological framework, the author narrowed the problems, classified the related items, and eliminated redundancy so that nine problem areas were addressed in the ASIMDC and Guidelines.

Because a cross-section of professionals in various parts of the country with varied backgrounds and disciplines were needed to validate the proposed model, the Delphi method was used to pool and bring together their opinions.[21] The Delphi method is a systematic use of opinion with group consensus through a use of a series of questionnaires which are used to elicit and refine the opinions from experts with professional training or training gained through disciplinary experience.[22-24]

The Delphi questionnaire consisted of 141 potential guideline items which required the panelists to determine the essentiality of each to the ideal pool program. Figure 1 is a sample of the questionnaire to which the panelists responded "yes" item is essential, "no" not essential, or "not familiar" enough to make a judgment. An 80% consensus from the panel of experts was set as criterion. A panel of 108 experts representing 11 disciplines validated the Guidelines for the ASIMDC. Discipline orientation of the panelists was as follows:

## Figure 1

GUIDELINES FOR PROPOSED AQUATIC MODEL OF SERVICE INTERVENTION FOR
HANDICAPPED CHILDREN

Level III ELEMENT:  ENVIRONMENTS are the unique characteristics and resources of a
physical and social setting which include home, medical-therapeutic,
educational, community, and the aquatic programming setting, including
the hydrosphere or pool

Level IV COMPONENT A:  ENVIRONMENTAL considerations are the resource and limiting
factors in the physical or social setting which influence the quality
of normal learning, development, treatment, and/or communication processes in the setting

Please evaluate the following Environmental Subcomponents with regard to the ideal
aquatic program for handicapped children.

YES - essential to the model
NO - not essential to the model
NF - not familiar enough with the item to make an expert judgement

| YES | NO | NF | Level V-A-ENVIRONMENTAL SUBCOMPONENTS | Comments |
|---|---|---|---|---|
| | | | 1. Physical environmental subcomponents are the characteristic features of the environment itself; consisting first of the facility, and second, of the pool and water, and should include considerations of the following: a. Physical factors of the facility which should be considered include: * accessibility of entry to and inside the building * size and type of pool, e.g., inside, outdoor, above-ground, etc. * permanent and moveable equipment for pool entry and exit * advantages/disadvantages of having observation windows | |
| | | | b. Emotional factors that a child associates with the physical environment, e.g., lack of accessibility, fear of the water or some aspect of the pool, excitement | |
| | | | c. Intensity and quality of stimuli related to the child's needs, e.g., a hyperactive child's problems intensifying in a noisy, active pool | |
| | | | d. Physical factors of the water influencing position and mobility in the water (e.g., buoyancy, turbulence, temperature, or quality of the chemicals in the water) | |
| | | | 2. Aspects of the child's social environments which may influence the child's function in the aquatic environment include: a. parental or primary caretaker's involvement and cooperation in other ecosystems, e.g., is school, in therapy, or at home, especially with home aquatic activities to reinforce pool programming activities and goals | |
| | | | b. school social environment including: 1) type of classroom, e.g., self-contained, categorical, special or mainstreamed class | |
| | | | 2) teacher participation with child in aquatic program itself and/or with classroom activities to reinforce aquatic activities or goals | |
| | | | 3) educational goals, social service and psychological goals | |
| | | | e. Medical-therapeutic social environment service information e.g., type of therapy and therapist, treatment goals, location, frequency, progress made, cooperation with therapist | |
| YES | NO | NF | | Comments |
| | | | d. Interpersonal aspects of the social environment that influence the quality of the child's development and learning, including: 1. communication and interpersonal relationships between the child and adult/teacher/therapist and motivation provided to the child for learning | |
| | | | 2. recreational or therapeutic discipline orientation or training which influence cooperation and attitude differences within staff relationships or interactions between the child and staff | |
| | | | 3. The biological aspect of the Environmental component is the anatomical, physiological, and neurodevelopmental make-up of the individual child. Considerations of the child's internal environment are: a. physical ability and disabilities, range of motion, strength, orthopedic status, tone, body type | |
| | | | b. internal interferences with individual's learning or cognitive developmental processes, e.g., perceptual dysfunction | |
| | | | c. child's ability to provide own internal motivation for learning and development or to respond to motivating stimuli | |
| | | | d. child's abilities to cope with the environment by adapting or making internal changes to maintain homeostasis (e.g., keeping warm in a cold pool) in response to the external social or physical environment | |

Comments: _____

Are there any other Environmental Subcomponents that should be considered? If yes, describe: _____

Are any of the subcomponents misplaced under the Environmental Component? If yes, where should they be placed? _____

- Recreational/Instructional Professionals = 28 panelists (included adapted physical educators, aquatic directors or instructors and participants, special education teachers)
- Therapeutic Professionals = 49 panelists (included physical therapists, physicians, occupational therapists, speech pathologists, nurses)
- Integrated Professionals = 33 panelists (included administrators, recreational therapists, university faculty, mixed other disciplines)

## LEVELS OF THE MODEL AND THE DIRECTION OF THE DERIVATION

The intent of the 1981 Dulcy[16] study was to construct a normative ASIMDC and design normative Guidelines for use as prescriptive strategies for overcoming problems in aquatic programs for disabled children. The following theoretical bases were incorporated as the basic premises of the model and subsequent Guidelines: learning, development, ecology, and treatment. Other constructs included concepts of transdisciplinary professional approaches and cross-environmental transfer of learning and professional roles. Each of the prescriptive components of the model are normative, or strategies aimed at narrowing the gap between the current and desired situations.[19]

The five-level ASIMDC is presented in Figure 2. The ASIMDC is constructed so that each level reflects, and is derived from, the supraceding level, as indicated by the arrows on the figure.

Realizing that all the ecological elements (people, processes, and environments) are common to the archetype Service Intervention Models, ecological theory is selected as the primary framework for ASIMDC development. Level II is comprised of the Service Intervention Models themselves: the Home, Educational, Medical-Therapeutic, and Aquatic Programs, all which are based upon the Theoretical Bases of Level I. In Level III, each of the traditional Service Intervention Models from Level II is further delineated into ecological contributions to the aquatic model of People, Processes, and Environmental Elements. The Service Intervention Processes of Level III are essential connections between the various service delivery models and the aquatic environment, facilitating integration of the two. Ecological Processes are probably more responsible than any other part for the effectiveness of the ASIMDC.

From each ecological element is derived the Components of Level IV, and the detailed Guidelines validated by the study, or the Subcomponents, of Level V. In order that the aquatic ecosystem be a normative ecosystem, constraints must be applied to the ecological framework and to Levels III and IV. Safety and Legal Constraints and their derived subconstraints are placed on Levels III, IV, and V.

FIGURE 2

AQUATIC SERVICE INTERVENTION MODEL FOR DISABLED CHILDREN

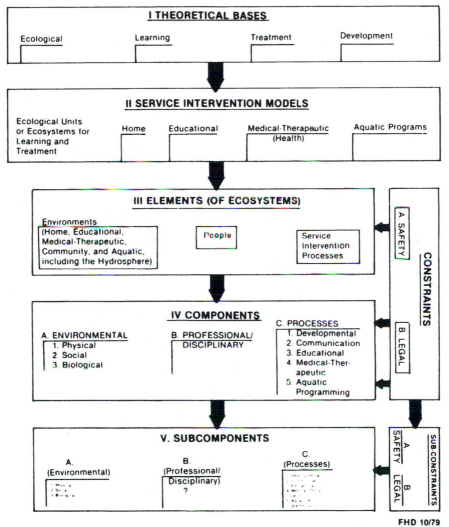

FHD 10/79

## RESULTS: VALIDATION OF THE MODEL
## FRAMEWORK & GUIDELINES

Guidelines related to each of the five levels of the ASIMDC proposed for use in the ideal aquatic program were integrated throughout the questionnaire. Of the original 141 Guideline items, 139 (98.6%) were considered vital to the ideal program by the criterion 80% of the panelists.

On further analysis of the criterion consensus, 86.5% of the items were approved at the 90-100% consensus level, 12% at the 80-89% consensus level, and 0.7% each (or one item each) at the 70-79% and the 50-59% levels respectively. A 100% consensus of the panelists was obtained on 8 items of 5.6% of the items. The panelists reached a 99% consensus on 32 items or 22.7% of the items.

As panelists reached the criterion consensus on all but two of these items, each of the five levels of the ASIMDC was validated as an essential part. The consensus validation of the Guidelines also simultaneously validated the framework of the ecological ASIMDC almost totally as proposed: an integrated, transdisciplinary approach to aquatic intervention. Because of the high consensus of the panelists, the validated ASIMDC and Guidelines are highly usable,[24] with the exception of the two non-consensus items. The panelists' comments on the fact that "the study was badly needed" seemed to acknowledge the existence and relevance of both the problems and of the proposed Guideline strategies.

Mean consensus on the subcomponents and subconstraints ranged from 93-98% in all areas except the Environmental Subcomponents, which reached 83% (Figure 3). The relatively low mean consensus on the Environmental Subcomponents was primarily the effect of the two non-consensus items. The two Environmental Subcomponent nonconsensus items related to social environmental considerations of the child's type of classroom and the classroom teacher's participation in the aquatic program itself, or in reinforcing aquatic activities in the classroom. Safety Constraints, Medical-Therapeutic Process Subcomponents, Communication and Aquatic Programming Process Subcomponents and Legal Constraints received the four highest mean consensus.

The paragraphs to follow describe the essential parts of the ASIMDC validated by the criterion consensus of the panel of experts.

## Level I: Theoretical Bases of: Ecology, Learning, Development, and Treatment

Level I includes the Theoretical Bases used in model development and in planning and in implementing an aquatic program. The panelists validated the theoretical bases of the aquatic model: ecological theory,[1] developmental theory,[2,25] learning theory[11,12,13] and treatment theory.[2,26,27,28] Although single theories have been used in unidisciplinary aquatic programs (e.g., treatment theory in therapeutic programs), the four theories have not been used in combination. Ecological and developmental theory are fairly uncommon to aquatic programs, however, inclusion of these theoretical bases was approved. In addition, although some programs apply treatment[29,30] and learning theory[9,31,32,33]

FIGURE 3

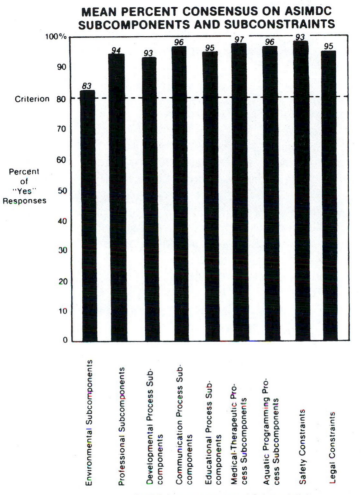

FIGURE 3

**MEAN PERCENT CONSENSUS ON ASIMDC SUBCOMPONENTS AND SUBCONSTRAINTS**

such application in aquatic programs is not currently universal, nor are these theories traditionally used in combination with the others.

## Level II: The Service Intervention Models of Home, Education, Treatment, and Aquatic Programming

Level II of the validated ASIMDC is comprised of Service Intervention Models which are derived from each Theoretical Base. The panelists validated the Home, Educational, Medical-Therapeutic, and Aquatic Program ecosystems, or the disabled child's learning and treatment ecosystems, as described by Apter.[1] Developmental, home-based intervention models are presented by several authors[2,3,34,35] and are based upon learning and developmental theory. Educational service intervention models[1,5] have learning theory[11,12,13] as their bases. These service educational models may now be applied to the aquatic environment as well.

Treatment theory is applied primarily in the medical-therapeutic environment, but is also applied in educational,[36] hydrotherapeutic,[29,30,37] and home intervention models.[38] Several treatment models also involve treatment theory along with ecological theory.[2,4-6,39,40] These ecosystems have common elements with the aquatic environment and, therefore, according to ecological theory,[1] may influence the child's behavior in the aquatic program. Guideline questions relating to the four Service Intervention Models were integrated throughout the ASIMDC and Guidelines. The people and processes involved with each of these settings all contribute to the aquatic environment. Transference and integration of the professionals' roles, theories, methods, and processes promote the maximum carryover between settings.

### Level III: Elements of the Ecosystem: Environments, People, and Service Intervention Processes

which become

### Level IV: Components and Level V: Subcomponents: Environments, Professional/Disciplinary, and Processes

1. Developmental
2. Communication
3. Education
4. Medical-Therapeutic
5. Aquatic Programming

and

### Level IV: Constraints and Level V: Subconstraints: Safety and Legal

Validation of the first three levels of the ASIMDC was not directly obtained through consensus on specific questionnaire items. Instead, panelist consensus was obtained on some Guidelines and from general Component and Constraint areas of the Guidelines. As an example, the Educational Subcomponents (Figure 1, Level V, C,3) delineate the Educational Process Subcomponents (Level IV), one of the ecological process Elements (Level III), a part of the Educational Service Intervention Model used in a school (Level II) which is based on the Learning Theory (Level I). Items reflecting each of the Theoretical Bases were included in the Subcomponents throughout the Guidelines. In addition, the entire Educational Process, Medical-Therapeutic Process, and Developmental Process Subcomponent areas are based upon learning, treatment, and developmental theory, respectively. Specific Guideline items and details on supportive information may be found in the 1981 Dulcy study.[16]

## IMPLICATIONS OF THE VALIDATED AQUATIC SERVICE INTERVENTION MODEL AND GUIDELINES

By offering prescriptive Guideline solutions to the identified problems, the integrated, transdisciplinary ASIMDC framework and accompanying Guidelines were intended to be an impetus enhancing professional practice and increasing the meaningfulness and effectiveness of aquatic programs for disabled children.

Hopefully the impact of an ideal model will be quite broad, so that ultimately the safety and function of the individual disabled child within the aquatic programs are improved. Both the shortcomings and benefits of aquatic programs influence the many people who function in the multiple aquatic programming environments. Several panelists recommended simplifying the language used in the Guidelines to facilitate transdisciplinary use in establishing new programs or improving existing programs. These Guidelines may provide professionals with a starting place in aquatic programming and with an outline from which to work.

The ASIMDC Guidelines integrating transdisciplinary programmatic approaches could be useful to both recreationally oriented and therapeutically-oriented aquatic agencies, professional staff, and students in professional fields involved with aquatics. Authors and editors of training manuals for recreational adapted aquatic and YMCA program instructors[31-33] have requested additional therapeutic input both directly into their programs and indirectly into publications for future revisions.

Public Law 94-142[14] has created a need for more professionals than ever to deliver educational and related services to disabled children. Many professionals who work with disabled children are now also involved in adapted aquatic programs, frequently within educational programs. Students and professionals who are preparing to work in educational environments, as well as professionals who now work in these settings, need information and methods in aquatics for the disabled. In order to maximize each child's full potential, professional resources and time must be carefully planned for optimal use. Efficiency involves developing methods of alternative treatment and sharing of professional management skills. The Guidelines and ASIMDC may provide such a framework with which to build this needed supplemental treatment and educational media.

The essential considerations in development of aquatic programs may also be used as outline for professional training curricula for both therapists and aquatic instructors. As noted in the 1981 study,[16] only a small percentage of aquatic training was obtained from professional curricula. Instead, professionals received training in aquatics either through nationally established professional training workshops or from employment or work experiences. A portion of preparatory curricula related to therapy in educational settings or to hydrotherapy could also adopt the Guidelines as a basis for curricula. Aquatic trained physical therapists entering the profession could use additional skills in their own treatments, more capably implement or provide consultation programs, or start new programs.

Comments on an Environmental Subcomponent in the questionnaire indicated that teacher (special education) preparation in aquatics is also needed. The competency-based curricula for teachers of the handicapped[41] includes aquatics as a part of the suggested curricula and competencies for teachers of the handicapped. Instructional packages would promote a more widespread distribution of the material and instruction.

National and regional programs have increased their workshop offerings in aquatics in response to professional demands and needs. National conferences of associations such as the American Physical Therapy Association, American Association on Mental Deficiencies and Council for Exceptional Children have offered presentations on aquatic programs for disabled children. Continuing education presentations are available on a regular basis from several institutions. At least one program in physical therapy regularly includes aquatic learning experiences as a supplemental approach for working with children in educational environments. In the past six years, at least seven items relating to aquatics have appeared in an information sharing newsletter for physical therapists.[42] Program guidelines identified in this study could be used to answer these programmatically related requests.

Intradisciplinary practice may also be influenced by the development of the ASIMDC and Guidelines. Physical therapists with specialties not only in pediatrics, but also in orthopedics, neurological disorders, community health, cardiopulmonary, and sports medicine areas may, at times, use adaptive aquatics in their patient management. With training in the necessary knowledge and skill areas, physical therapists could increase their input into recreational programs. Increased input could decrease the frustration of working without specific goals and improve the attitudinal environment for aquatic programs. The available training methods and materials of both recreational and therapeutic approaches to aquatics may be supplemented by these additional transdisciplinary aquatic methods, rationales for pool use, and specific methods for children with various disabilities. Additional first-hand experiences using these methods might motivate American allied health and aquatic professionals to initiate more accurate and complete interdisciplinary documentation and instructional materials.

American professionals hopefully will be motivated to research and document the effectiveness of the Guidelines and ASIMDC and of individual test model programs for all ages. Clinical research documentation of individual programs would provide statistical and clinical evidence to school, professional, and aquatic administrators.

The transdisciplinary Guidelines which address the specific problem areas in aquatics can perhaps motivate and direct the cooperation of service delivery teams toward greater involvement and support in aquatic programs. In order to heighten interest and involvement in aquatics, the interested panelists, other professionals, and parents could be approached to collaborate and form an alliance similar to that existing in the British Commonwealth.[43] Cooperation and communication with the established British organization could provide support and motivation for success in both the initiation and continuation of the newly formed American group.

The author believes that professional interest in effective aquatic programs will enhance, reinforce, and coordinate learning and treatment for all the disabled child's other ecosystems. Perhaps therapeutic pools will not go unused. The desired ultimate consequence would be to improve the quality of practices of both individual personnel and of aquatic programs in general.

## RECOMMENDATIONS FOR FUTURE RESEARCH

Several additional analyses could determine the full extent of the apparent dichotomy between recreational and therapeutic programs. A future study which controls the background information on panelists to a greater extent than done originally could provide data for statistical analysis. On the questionnaire, the panelists identified the orientation of their professional training in aquatics, as well as their discipline. These two items were categorized individually, as well as into a "combined discipline and training orientation." Each Guideline item also had a "Not Familiar" (NF) response category indicating that the panelist was not sufficiently familiar with the item to determine the essentiality of the item to the ideal program.

An indepth analysis of the NF response categories, items with a particular recreation or therapeutic slant, and the nonconsensus items could be used to determine the relationships between the traditional area of training for each discipline and approach and the NF responses, the slanted items, and the nonconsensus items. The analysis might empirically document the extent of the previously discussed dichotomy between recreational and therapeutic programs in educational and in clinical practices. Educational needs could then be determined for each discipline orientation. Based on the Guidelines, competencies and curricula could be developed. Educational research could focus on various approaches for teaching the Guidelines as preparation for developing competency of both students and practicing therapists.

Responses marked NF could be analyzed to determine the extent to which the orientation of the discipline affects the knowledge regarding certain items. In addition, items with a particular recreational or therapeutic slant could be analyzed according to "discipline orientation" and "combined orientation" in order to determine the training influence.

Language simplification and further development of the Guidelines for the ASIMDC may be researched in a variety of ways. First, program details may be constructed for each level of the ASIMDC. For example, theoretical bases and professional methods may be detailed and expanded. Validation again may be performed through the use of the Delphi technique with an interdisciplinary panel of experts. Second, additional guidelines or considerations may be delineated for use with these already-validated Guidelines. These newly developed guidelines could aid the necessary decision-making regarding maximum program benefit while using less than the ideal situations and limited resources. These second guidelines would provide more tangible suggestions to those panelists critical of the idealism of the ASIMDC and Guidelines. Third, standards may be developed for evaluation of the ideal aquatic program itself, since the current Guidelines are intended only for program planning and implementation. Fourth, after development of evaluation guidelines and detailed model programs, demonstration model programs could be instituted.

Clinical research based on the ASIMDC could be done in a variety of ways. The effects of individual programs could be tested. Results of the ideal program could be compared with either recreational programs or therapeutic programs in isolation. Clinical research could also document the use of aquatics as an adjunct to other therapeutic or developmental techniques, in addition to the carryover effects of aquatic programming into the child's other ecosystems.

Experts in the British Commonwealth, where aquatics is used more widely than it is in the United States could expand upon the present research, on the ASIMDC and Guidelines. The result could be further expansion and detailing of the present information and data, as well as improved validity for these Guidelines. Comparisons of American and British responses would have implications for further delineation of areas and strategies for planning and implementing programs in the United States.

## CONCLUSIONS

Validation by a high degree of consensus of experts in aquatic programs has resulted in Guidelines and an Aquatic Service Intervention Model for Disabled Children which have both practical and research implications. Panelist consensus that an integrated program is ideal, implies that, as proposed, problems in unidisciplinary recreational or therapeutic programs may be overcome with a program that is transdisciplinary in approach. The comprehensive nature of the validated ASIMDC and Guidelines thus defines in ecological terms, a framework for transdisciplinary professional practices and training and a total integrated approach to the disabled child in aquatic programs.

## REFERENCES

1. Apter SJ: Applications of ecological theory: Towards a community special education model. *Except Child* 43:366-375, 1977.

2. Banus BS: *The Developmental Therapist.* Thorofare NJ, Charles C Slack, 1971.

3. Bijou SW: Practical implications of an interactional model of child development. *Except Child* 44:6-14, 1977.

4. Sternat J, Messina R, Nietupski J, et al: Integrated vs isolated therapy model. Occupational and physical therapy services for severely handicapped students: Toward a naturalized public school service delivery model. In Sontag E (ed): *Educational Programming for the Severe and Profoundly Handicapped.* Reston VA, A Special Publication of the Division of Mental Retardation, The Council for Exceptional Children, 1977.

5. Thomas ED, Marshall M: Clinical evaluation and coordination of services: An ecological model. *Except Child* 44:16-22, 1977.

6. Pearson PH, Williams CE (eds): *Physical Therapy Services in the Developmental Disabilities.* Springfield IL, Charles C Thomas, 1972.

7. West WL: The occupational therapist's changing responsibility to the community. *AJOT* 21:312, 1967.

8. Hutchinson D: The transdisciplinary approach. In Curry, Preppe (eds): *Mental Retardation: Nursing Approaches to Care.* CV Mosby, 1974, pp. 42-45.

9. American Association for Health, Physical Education, and Recreation: *A Practical Guide for Teaching the Mentally Retarded to Swim.* Washington, DC, YMCA, 1969.

10. Mason C: Pool activities with the multiply handicapped child. *Nursing Mirror* 25:50-52, 1975.

11. Gagne RM: *Essentials for Instruction.* Hinsdale IL, Dryden Press, 1974.

12. Robb MD: *The Dynamics of Motor Skill Acquisition.* Englewood Cliffs NJ, Prentice Hall, 1972.

13. Tyler R: *Basic Principles of Curriculum and Instruction.* Chicago, The University of Chicago Press, 1949.

14. Bureau of Education for the Handicapped. The education for all handicapped children act of 1975: PL 94-142; 20 USC 1401 et seq: *Federal Register* 42 (163): 42474-42518, August 23, 1977.

15. Dunn JM: Handicapped legislation and the public agency. In *New Horizons in Aquatics.* Council on National Cooperation of Aquatics, 1978, pp 63-66.

16. Dulcy FH: Essential Considerations for an Integrated, Developmental Aquatic Program Model for School-Aged Disabled Children. Masters thesis, Atlanta, Emory University, 1981.

17. Dulcy FH: Survey of educational needs of personnel working in aquatics for the handicapped. Park Forest South IL, 1976.

18. Kauffman RA: *Educational System Planning*. Englewood Cliffs NJ, Prentice Hall, 1972.

19. Sutherland JW: Architecting the future: A Delphi-based paradigm for normative system building. In Linstone HP, Turoff M (eds): *The Delphi Method*. Reading MA, Addison-Wesley Publishing Co., 1975, pp 463-486.

20. Black M: Models and archetypes. In Browdy HS, Ennis RH, Krimerman LI: *Philosophies of Educational Research*. New York, John Wiley and Sons, 1973, pp 474-482.

21. Moscovie I, Armstrong P, Shortells, Bennetti R: Health services research for decision makers: The use of the Delphi technique to determine health priorities, *J Health Politics, Policy and Law* 2:388-410, 1977.

22. Helmer O: *The Delphi Method for Systematizing Judgements about the Future (MR61)*. Los Angeles, Institute of Government and Public Affairs, 1966.

23. Helmer O: *Social Technology*. New York, Basic Books, 1966.

24. Linstone HP, Turoff M (eds): *The Delphi Method*. Reading MA, Addison-Wesley Publishing Co., 1975.

25. McGraw MB: *The Neurodevelopmental Maturation of the Human Infant*. New York, Hafner Publishing, 1969.

26. Ayres AJ: *Sensory Integration and Learning Disorders*. Los Angeles, Western Psychological Services, 1972.

27. Bobath, K, Bobath B: The neurodevelopmental approach to treatment. In Pearson PH, Williams CE (eds): *Physical Therapy Services in the Developmental Disabilities*. Springfield IL, Charles C Thomas, 1972, pp 114-136.

28. Knott M, Voss DE: *Proprioceptive Neuromuscular Facilitation, Patterns, and Techniques (2nd ed.)*. New York, Harper and Row, 1968.

29. Duffield MH (ed): *Exercise in Water*. Baltimore, Williams and Wilkins, 1976.

30. Lowman CL, Roen SG: *Therapeutic Use of Pools and Tanks*, Philadelphia, WB Saunders, 1952.

31. American Red Cross: *Methods in Adapted Aquatics: A Manual for the Instructor*. Washington DC, 1977.

32. American Red Cross: *Swimming for Persons with Physical and Mental Impairments*. Washington DC, 1977.

33. Reynolds G (ed): *A Swimming Program for the Handicapped*. New York, Associated Press (National Board of YMCA), 1973.

34. Campbell SK: Facilitation of cognitive and motor development in infants with central nervous system dysfunction. *Phys Ther* 54:346-353, 1974.

35. Campbell SK, Wilson JM: Planning infant learning programs. *Phys Ther* 562:1347-1357, 1976.

36. deHaven GE: Is selective hearing an occupational hazard in physical therapy? *Phys Ther* 54:1301-1304, 1974.

37. Harris SR: Neurodevelopmental treatment approach for teaching swimming to cerebral palsied children. *Phys Ther* 58:979-983, 1978.

38. Finnie NR: *Handling the Young Cerebral Palsied Child at Home (2nd ed)*. New York, EP Hutton Co., 1975.

39. Newman BJ, Young RJ: A model for teaching total person approach to patient problems. *Nurs Res* 21:265-269, 1972.

40. Smilkstein G: A model for teaching comprehensive health care, *J Med Educ* 52:773-775, 1957.

41. Connor FD, Rusalem H, Baken JW (eds): *Professional Preparation of Educators of Crippled Children: Competency-Based Programming Report on Special Study Institute*. Columbia University, Office of Education, 1971.

42. *Every Inch and a Half*. Toledo OH, The Jobst Institute, Inc.

43. Swimming for the disabled. *Br Med J* 1:6024:1489, 1976.

# Neonatal Hydrotherapy:
# An Adjunct to Developmental Intervention in an Intensive Care Nursery Setting

Jane K. Sweeney, MS, RPT

**ABSTRACT.** The use of hydrotherapy for high risk neonates in an intensive care nursery is described. Results of a pilot study to measure the changes in behavioral state and in the physiologic parameters of blood pressure and heart rate with aquatic intervention are presented. The risk-benefit relationship of the effects of hydrotherapy is discussed in terms of potential physiologic complications to high risk infants versus therapeutic neuromusculoskeletal and behavioral benefits.

Hydrotherapy has been used as a traditional therapeutic modality by health care providers in a variety of settings and for an extensive range of medical conditions. Its origin can be traced to Hippocrates (460-375 BC) who prescribed hot and cold contrast baths in the management of a variety of disease processes and to the Romans who popularized recreational and curative baths with total body immersion.[1] Historically, water has had highly effective use in rehabilitation programs by physical therapists as a medium for exercise in hydrotherapy tanks or in swimming pools.

The purpose of this article is to describe the use of hydrotherapy for infants at high risk for neurological impairment and developmental delay in an intensive care nursery setting. Results of a pilot study of physiological parameters (blood pressure and heart rate) and behavioral state changes before, during, and after aquatic intervention are presented.

Lieutenant Colonel Sweeney is a member of the Army Medical Specialist Corps currently assigned as a Special Project Officer in Pediatric Physical Therapy to the Department of Pediatrics, Madigan Army Medical Center (Box 369) Tacoma, WA 98431. She serves as High Risk Infant Project Director, Regional Pediatric Physical Therapy Consultant, and Clinical Specialty Advisor in Pediatric Physical Therapy to the Office of the Army Surgeon General. The author wishes to acknowledge the assistance of LTC Gary Pettett MD, Chief of Newborn Medicine and MAJ Carita Bird BS, RN, Nursery Supervisor, and express appreciation for their immeasurable support to the study.

## LITERATURE REVIEW

Although no studies addressing the use of water immersion in an intensive care nursery setting for management of abnormal muscle tone in premature or other infants at high risk for neurological impairment could be found, Harris describes spasticity inhibiting positions, movements, and water temperature using Neurodevelopmental Treatment (NDT) principles in swimming programs for cerebral palsied children.[2]

The use of hydrotherapy techniques in a neonatal intensive care unit to effect a behavioral state change to the quiet or active alert states in premature, medically stable infants who sleep or cry when handled has not been reported. Iles and McCrary, however, describe a reduction of crying and behavioral distress with increased infant-caregiver interaction during the use of "cuddle bathing" techniques in full term normal newborns.[3] "Cuddle bathing," a non-immersion method, first involves swaddling the infant in the supine position with a damp, warm towel. The infant is then washed segmentally from head to foot in the crib while maintaining eye contact with the care-provider. Leboyer subjectively reported the effectiveness of warm water immersion both in calming the newborn after the stresses of birth and in promoting infant-parent interaction and subsequent "bonding."[4]

Guidelines for teaching normal infants to swim have been previously outlined.[5, 6] The swimming reflex in normal infants was first described by McGraw who developed a three phase classification of aquatic behavior development: a) reflex swimming, b) disorganized motor activity, c) deliberate voluntary movements. These three phases were developed from 445 observations of 42 infants (11 days to 2 1/2 years of age) to identify the quality of amphibian movements used by children of varying ages during spontaneous prone propulsion through water without swimming instruction. McGraw interpreted these phases in the development of aquatic behavior to be a reflection of a transition from the reflexive neurological status of the neonate to the selective motor control of the toddler.[7, 8] The impact of practicing the swimming reflex in preparation for improved proficiency in infant swimming programs was not addressed.

## METHOD

### Patient Selection

The modality of hydrotherapy is judiciously used as an adjunct to an individualized developmental intervention program for high risk infants in the intensive care and intermediate care nurseries at Madigan Army Medical Center, Tacoma, Washington. In this program, the Brazelton Neonatal Behavioral Assessment Scale is implemented for evaluation of neuromuscular and behavioral status with interpretation of the clinical findings modified to the pre-term infant's gestational age.[9] The individualized sensory-motor and behavioral intervention program is then designed from the findings of the Brazelton Scale with the theory base, principles and goals of developmental intervention derived from the Neurodevelopmental Treatment Approach.[10, 11]

Indications for referral of medically stable infants to the hydrotherapy component of the developmental intervention program include the following:

a. Muscle tone abnormalities (hypertonus or hypotonus) affecting the quality and quantity of spontaneous movement and promoting the development of muscle group imbalance of excessive extension over flexion in the neck, trunk, or extremity regions (Figure 1).

b. Limitation of motion in the extremities related to muscular or connective tissue factors.

c. Behavioral state abnormalities: (1) Behavioral intolerance of graded "handling" (tactile, kinesthetic, vestibular, or proprioceptive facilitation/inhibition) to normalize muscle tone. (2) Excessive drowsiness during "handling" preventing social interaction with care-givers and the environment and contributing to depression of developmental reflexes and postural tone.

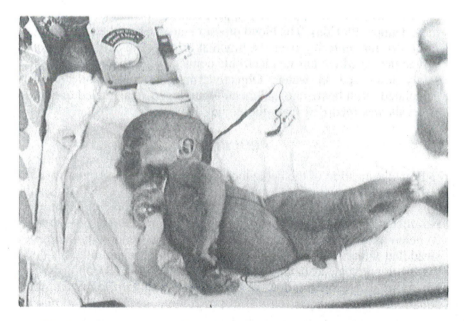

FIGURE 1. Hypertonic infant (Case 1) demonstrating excessive extension posturing

## Sample Data

Three subjects were selected from the Pediatric Physical Therapy caseload in the Neonatal Intensive Care Unit (NICU) at Madigan Army Medical Center to participate in the pilot study during the period of March-April 1982. Randomization was not used in the selection process; rather, the total patient load was screened for *medically stable* infants with abnormalities in muscle tone or in behavioral state control when handled. Infants were labeled "Medically Stable" when ventilator equipment and intravenous lines (IV) were discontinued and resolution of temperature instability and apnea/bradycardia episodes were demonstrated. Infants were not excluded from the study on the basis of sex, race, socio-economic background, diagnosis, or age. Table 1 illustrates the demographic data of the subjects.

## Equipment

A standard plastic bassinet was selected as the neonatal hydrotherapy tub. The water temperature was prepared at 99-101°F (37.2-38.3°C) after the tub had been scrubbed with betadine solution. An overhead radiant heater was placed over the tub to decrease temperature loss in the undressed infant, thereby promoting thermoregulation and maximizing inhibition of hypertonus during "handling" techniques in warm water.

Mean blood pressure and heart rate were electronically measured by the DINAMAPP Neonatal Vital Signs Monitor (Model 847 by Critikon, Inc., Tampa, Florida). The blood pressure cuff was applied to the infant's right arm for centering over the brachial artery. The cuff is a pneumatic driven device which has no electronic connection to the infant and can be safely immersed in water. Objective measurement of electronically calculated mean heart rate and mean blood pressure at cycled one minute intervals was recorded from the digital display.

## PROCEDURE

For investigation of the behavioral and physiological responses of high risk infants to aquatic intervention, a three part data collection method was implemented. The first part involved documentation of the three parameters of 1) mean heart rate, 2) mean blood pressure and 3) behavioral state. These measurements were recorded on dressed, swaddled infants in the sidelying position at five minute intervals during the 20 minute period *before* the aquatic intervention. Second, the three parameters were recorded at five minute intervals *during* the ten minute aquatic intervention session. Third, the three parameters were again recorded at five minute intervals during the twenty minute period im-

| | CHRONOLOGICAL AGE | CORRECTED AGE | BIRTH WEIGHT | SEX | DIAGNOSES |
|---|---|---|---|---|---|
| Case 1 | 5 Mo. | 2 1/2 Mo. | 1040 grams at 30 week gestation. | M | prematurity<br>bronchopulmonary dysplasia, Grade III<br>tracheomalacia<br>osteomyelitis right talus<br>hyperbilirubinemia<br>anemia |
| Case 2 | 3 Mo. | 3 Mo. | 2778 grams at 43 weeks gestation | M | neonatal asphyxia<br>dysmorphic facies<br>failure-to-thrive syndrome<br>pneumonia<br>profound bilateral sensori-neural hearing impairment |
| Case 3 | 2 Mo. | 34 weeks gestation | 820 grams at 26 weeks gestation. | F | prematurity<br>intraventricular hemorrhage, grade III<br>hydrocephalus<br>bronchopulmonary dysplasia, grade III<br>hyperbilirubinemia<br>sepsis<br>anemia |

TABLE I. Demographic Data of Subjects

mediately *after* the intervention. In this final period, the infants remained undressed but were again swaddled and placed in the side-lying position in the bassinet.

Two methods of aquatic intervention were implemented: 1) warm water immersion by one examiner, 2) warm water immersion and hydrotherapy techniques by two examiners (one at head/shoulder region and one at pelvis/lower extremity region). The hydrotherapy techniques involved midline positioning of the head, graded muscle tone normalizing movements of the trunk and extremities, and proximal hand placement (key points of control) consistent with the Neurodevelopmental Treatment Approach.[2, 10, 11]

The behavioral state of the infants was coded from the scoring system developed by T. Berry Brazelton, M.D. (Table 2). The evaluation and scoring of behavioral states are described in the Brazelton Neonatal Behavioral Assessment Scale.[9]

A total of twenty observations were recorded from the three infants. This resulted in a sum of 9 observations of water IMMERSION ONLY and 11 observations of water IMMERSION and HYDROTHERAPY. The frequency and type of aquatic intervention recorded from the three subjects are outlined below:

a. Case 1 - four IMMERSION ONLY sessions and six IMMERSION and HYDROTHERAPY sessions.
b. Case 2 - three IMMERSION ONLY sessions and three IMMERSION and HYDROTHERAPY sessions.
c. Case 3 - two IMMERSION ONLY sessions and two IMMERSION and HYDROTHERAPY sessions.

All infants were fed on a four hour schedule with data collection occurring one hour before feeding.


TABLE 2:    Behavioral States    (Brazelton Scale[9])

STATE 1:    Quiet sleep.

2:    Active sleep.

3:    Drowsiness/semi-dozing.

4:    Quiet alert.

5:    Active alert.

6:    Crying.

## RESULTS

Mean changes in the three parameters of heart rate, blood pressure, and behavioral state during aquatic intervention were calculated for each case. In addition, the combined mean values from all cases were established for each parameter. These values are illustrated in Figures 2-4.

Collective data trends from the three cases demonstrated the following: a) increased blood pressure, heart rate, and behavioral state during both forms of aquatic intervention; b) decreased heart rate after HYDRO-THERAPY with increased heart rate after the sessions of IMMERSION ONLY (baseline established twenty minutes prior to aquatic intervention); c) smaller increase in blood pressure after HYDROTHERAPY than after IMMERSION ONLY; d) maintenance of the "quiet alert" behavioral state after HYDROTHERAPY in contrast to the "drowsy" state following IMMERSION ONLY. HYDROTHERAPY utilizing NDT facilitation/inhibition principles with gentle graded flexion and rotary movements at shoulder and pelvic girdle regions with midline head position resulted in longer periods of sustained alertness and less change in physiologic variables than the ten minute sessions of warm water IMMERSION ONLY.

## DISCUSSION

These data clearly indicate a physiologic cost to high risk infants when aquatic intervention is utilized as a therapeutic modality in an intensive care nursery setting. This cost must be carefully evaluated in terms of each infant's general medical stability and individual heart rate and blood pressure patterns before hydrotherapy can safely be considered for inclusion in a developmental early intervention program during the inpatient phase. Medical clearance by neonatology and nursing staff, vital signs monitoring, and pre-established individual criteria for the maximal limits of each infant's blood pressure, heart rate, and acceptable color changes during hydrotherapy are essential requirements for risk management. Although normal physiologic values of blood pressure and heart rate have been reported for premature and full term neonates, the vital signs range with stimulation must be established for each infant in collaboration with the supervising neonatologist.[12, 13]

While acknowledging the physiologic risk, many clinical benefits were obtained when hydrotherapy was judiciously used in the newborn nursery. These benefits are outlined as follows:

a. *Improvement in Abnormal Muscle Tone:* The common posturing of hypertonic and hypotonic infants into excessive extension to stabilize of "fix" against the mattress was quickly eliminated during

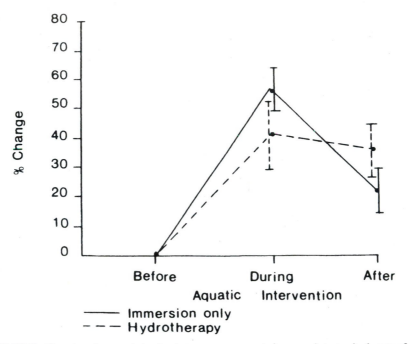

FIGURE 2. Alterations in mean behavioral state: mean percent change and ± standard error of the mean

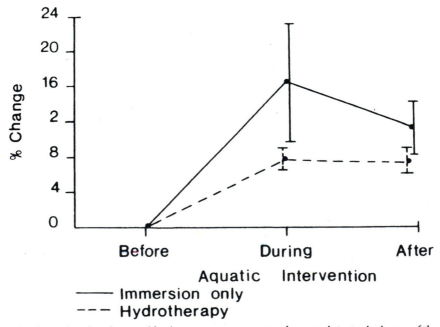

FIGURE 3. Alterations in mean blood pressure: mean percent change and ± standard error of the mean

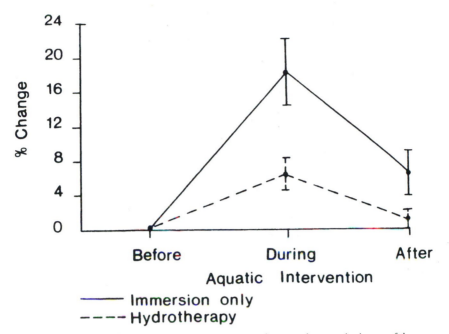

FIGURE 4. Alterations in mean heart rate: mean percent change and ± standard error of the mean

hydrotherapy. Elongation of neck and trunk extensor musculature, shoulder protraction, midline movements of arms, and posterior pelvic tilt with spontaneous kicking of legs were easily elicited. (Figure 5) The significantly improved semi-flexed posture and both quality and quantity of spontaneous movement were obtained with less time and effort by the examiner and higher behavioral tolerance by the infant than when a similar approach was used without the medium of water. Muscle tone changes were frequently maintained for two hours.

b. *Enhancement of Visual and Auditory Orientation Responses:* Prolonged high quality alertness and concomitant visual fixing and tracking of human faces, auditory localization of human voices, and longer periods of social interaction with caregivers were demonstrated during and after the HYDROTHERAPY as compared to warm water IMMERSION ONLY or general handling only.

c. *Improvement in Feeding Behavior:* In this study, hydrotherapy was scheduled one hour before scheduled feeding to prepare the infants for complete arousal and for flexed midline postural changes conducive to optimal feeding (Figure 6). The side effects of fatigue and temperature loss during hydrotherapy must be recognized and carefully monitored to prevent exhaustion of the infant and the subsequent need for gavage feeding.

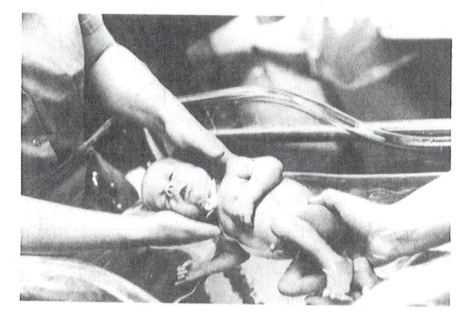

FIGURE 5. Normalization of abnormal muscle tone during hydrotherapy (Case 1)

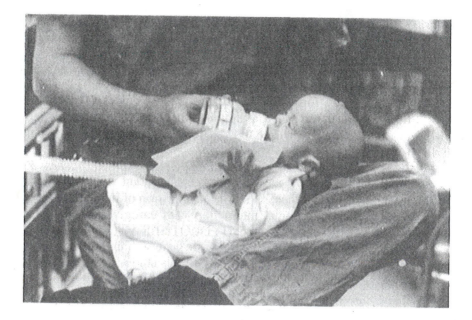

FIGURE 6. Semi-flexed midline feeding position after hydrotherapy (Case 1)

d. *Contracture Control:* Although limited joint motion was not clinically evident in the subjects of this study, warm water provides an optimal medium for the management of contractures. Mild flexion contractures (20-25) degrees in elbows and knees and dynamic hip adduction contractures can be safely and quickly eliminated by gentle muscle/joint mobilization and elongation techniques in warm water (Figure 7) as opposed to the traditional range of motion and stretching techniques frequently prescribed for adult orthopedic patients.

e. *Parent Participation:* Therapeutic bathing techniques were incorporated into the NICU parent teaching program (Figure 8). Early parent participation in the nursery was fostered in child care and in specific developmental activities during the inpatient period to prepare for carryover into the home environment at hospital discharge. This early pleasurable involvement of parent and child in hydrotherapy and bathing can provide a strong base for future participation in aquatics as a family recreational activity and if needed, as an adjunct to an out-patient developmental therapy program.

f. *Role Release to NICU Nursing Staff:* When oriented to treatment goals and trained in specific hydrotherapy techniques for individual infants, the NICU nursing staff can effectively carry on the

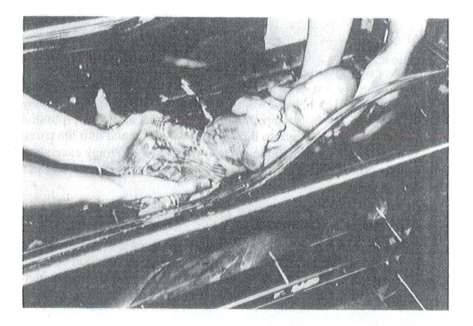

FIGURE 7. Results of hypertonus inhibition in hip adductor muscles during hydrotherapy

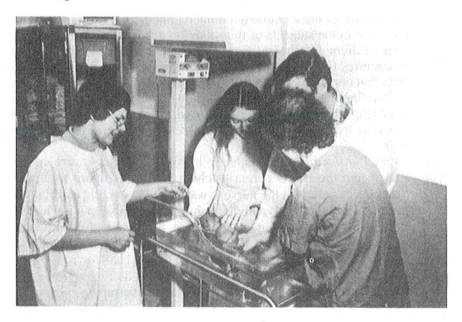

FIGURE 8. Parent participation in therapeutic bathing with assistance by neonatal nurse and supervision by pediatric physical therapist

hydrotherapy program established by the pediatric therapist. This release of the pediatric therapist's role to the neonatal nurse allows additional use of hydrotherapy on evening and night shifts and continued teaching and supervision of parents in therapeutic bathing when evening and weekend visiting patterns occur.

g. *Cost Effectiveness:* The use of equipment (tub, vital signs monitor) readily available in the newborn nursery, the short (10 minute) time period required for therapeutic effects, as well as the incorporation of therapeutic bathing into the nursing care plan and into the parent participation program in the nursery make hydrotherapy exceedingly cost effective in terms of equipment, time management, and personnel resources.

## IMPLICATIONS FOR FUTURE RESEARCH

Physiologic responses and behavioral state changes associated with the adjunctive use of hydrotherapy in developmental intervention for high risk neonates have been described. To quantitate these responses more precisely, design changes to accommodate a larger randomized sample of infants matched for gestational age and diagnosis with control groups of full term infants and premature infants with uncomplicated neonatal courses might be considered.

In future studies, a design which includes objective measurement of muscle tone and postural changes before and after hydrotherapy could validate the subjective muscle tone changes observed in the subjects of this study. An analysis of the swimming reflex in normal full term infants as compared to premature infants with discussion of possible significance to later swimming proficiency would add to the knowledge base of therapeutic aquatics.

## SUMMARY

The traditional therapeutic modality of hydrotherapy was modified for use in an intensive care setting for infants at high risk for neurological impairment and developmental delay. The physiologic responses and behavioral state changes of infants in a pilot study were measured before, during, and after aquatic intervention. An analysis of the risk-benefit relationship was presented in terms of physiologic risk to the infant versus therapeutic benefits of incorporating hydrotherapy into an inpatient developmental intervention program for high risk neonates and their parents.

With increasing populations of surviving infants at high risk for neuromuscular dysfunction, pediatric therapists can offer invaluable adjunctive diagnostic and therapeutic support in neurodevelopmental assessment and treatment as health care extenders in NICUs. While playing a major role in reinforcing the *preventive* aspects of health care by providing developmental early intervention to this high risk population and parents, pediatric therapists must carefully monitor the physiologic responses of pre-term infants to this intervention and diligently coordinate the developmental programming and long term follow-up with the intensive care nursing and medical staff.

## REFERENCES

1. Duffield MH (ed): *Exercise in Water.* New York, McMillan Publishing Co. Inc, 1976.
2. Harris SR: Neurodevelopmental treatment approach for teaching swimming to cerebral palsied children. *Phys Ther* 58:979-83, 1978.
3. Iles JP, McCrary, M: Cuddle bathing can be fun. *Canad Nurse* 73:24-27, 1977.
4. Leboyer F: *Birth Without Violence.* New York, Alfred A. Knopf, 1975.
5. Prudden B: *Your Baby Can Swim.* Stockbridge, Aquarian Press, 1978.
6. Timmermans C: *How to Teach Your Baby to Swim.* New York, Stein & Day, 1975.
7. McGraw MB: Swimming behavior of the human infant. *J Pediatr* 15:485-90, 1939.
8. McGraw MB: *Neuromuscular Maturation of the Human Infant.* New York, Hafner Publishing Co, 1963.
9. Brazelton TB: *Neonatal Behavioral Assessment Scale,* publication 50. Clinics in Developmental Medicine, Philadelphia, JB Lippincott Co, 1973.
10. Bobath B, Bobath K: The neurodevelopmental treatment of cerebral palsy. *Phys Ther* 47:1039-41, 1967.

11. Bobath B, Bobath K: Cerebral palsy, in Pearson PH, Williams CE (eds): *Physical Therapy Services in the Developmental Disabilities,* ed3. Springfield, Charles C. Thomas, 1976.

12. Avery GB (ed): *Neonatology,* ed 2. Philadelphia, JB Lippincott Co, 1981.

13. Pierog SH, Ferrara A: *Medical Care of the Sick Newborn.* Saint Louis, CV Mosby Co, 1976.

# The Use of Water as a Modality to Treat an Infant with Mild Neurological Dysfunction: A Case Report

Susan Attermeier, MACT, LPT

**ABSTRACT.** The use of water was integrated into therapy for an infant with mild neurological dysfunction, with favorable results. A description of the techniques is presented, along with a possible rationale for their success.

## INTRODUCTION

Treatment of infants with neurological dysfunction focuses on supporting the development of appropriate posture and movement while minimizing abnormal patterns. To this end, parents are instructed in techniques of handling and positioning as well as appropriate play activities. This article describes a child with whom treatment in water was used to elicit specific motor responses in the context of the home program. A possible rationale for the success of this approach, along with general implications for early intervention, is presented.

## BIRTH HISTORY

Emily was born two weeks prematurely, the pregnancy having been complicated by a gestational diabetes which was difficult to control. Apgar scores were 8 at 1 minute and 9 at 5 minutes. At birth the blood sugar was 45 mg% and glucose was administered intravenously for 26 hours. The hypoglycemia resolved and Emily was discharged from the

Ms. Attermeier currently is Assistant Professor, Department of Medical Allied Health Professions, Division of Physical Therapy, University of North Carolina at Chapel Hill. She also is the Section Head, Physical Therapy, Division for Disorders of Development and Learning, University of North Carolina at Chapel Hill, Chapel Hill, NC 27514.

The development of this paper was supported in part by the US Public Health Service, Maternal and Child Health Services Project Grant No. 916, and by grant No. HD-03110 from the National Institute of Child Health and Human Development.

hospital after 5 days. Her mother had become concerned on the first postnatal day when she could elicit head turning and visual attending to the right but not to the left. Shortly thereafter she noted decreased movements of the left arm and leg and entrapment of the left thumb. The asymmetries were also apparent to her pediatrician, and when they were still present at 3 1/2 months of age a referral was made for physical therapy.

## EVALUATION RESULTS

At four months of chronological age (CA), Emily began receiving biweekly physical therapy with diligent home programming. Her evaluation results soon showed that she was developing at an accelerated rate. Her initial score on the Motor Scale of the Bayley Scales of Infant Development (BSID) was average, but starting at 6 months (CA) her scores ranged between 2 and 3 standard deviations above the mean for both chronological and adjusted age (AA). Administration of the mental scale of the BSID at 7 months CA yielded similar results.

The initial motor examination revealed a number of asymmetries. Emily consistently turned and tilted her head more to the right than to the left. Hand sucking and reaching were more frequent on the right. Both thumbs were adducted, the left to a greater extent than the right. The pelvis was swung to the left and kicking excursion was diminished on the left. Ankle dorsiflexion combined with leg extension was diminished on the left. Response to tactile stimulation was better on the right. Plantar grasp was present bilaterally but was exaggerated on the left.

### First Treatment Phase (4 to 5 1/2 months CA)

During this period therapy was geared toward supporting and correcting activities in the supine and prone positions. In the supine position, tactile stimuli were used to elicit left foot and toe movements with the leg in varying degrees of flexion and extension. Head-turning to the left and mouthing of the left hand were encouraged. Small diameter rattles were placed in the web space of the left hand to promote thumb abduction. Passive trunk elongation in supine and side-lying were followed by placement in prone, and elicitation of symmetrical trunk extension.

As Emily began to reach consistently with the left arm, she showed poorly dissociated scapulo-humeral movement with a slight tendency toward internal rotation and pronation. This was corrected by manual stabilization of the scapula and placement of desired toys such that reaching patterns combined external rotation with both pronation and supination. For example: At this stage of development Emily placed all grasped objects in her mouth. In order to utilize this urge, toys and rattles with tubular handles about 1/2 inch in diameter were presented, with emphasis on the left side. They were presented so that in order to reach them Emily had to turn her head and position her shoulder in extension, abduction and external rotation. From this position, varying degrees of elbow extension, forearm supination and finger extension could be obtained by moving the toy. The scapula was prevented from moving during the first part of a reaching pattern, in order to promote mobility of the humerus on the scapula. The toy would then be positioned so that in order to grasp it Emily had to pronate her forearm. She would subsequently supinate in order to mouth it. Within any single treatment session, this activity was initiated in side lying and repeated until no abnormalities were noted. This was followed by work in supine and finally in prone. By following this pattern Emily first practiced moving with little gravitational resistance, then with progressively more resistance.

Emily's mother integrated all these activities in daily routines, including bathtime. During bathing, special attention was also paid to providing increased sensory input. The whole body, but especially the left side, was rubbed with soap, sponges, and towels. The face, palms of the hands and soles of the feet were given extra stimulation though never in such a way as to elicit protective or withdrawal responses.

In the second week of treatment, Emily's mother reported that she was having noticeably better success in obtaining good motor patterns during bathtime when Emily was placed in warm water. Because Emily enjoyed water play and her mother could clearly observe a difference in motor behavior, bathtime was a pleasurable experience for both. In order to maximize motor gains, two bathing periods per day, each lasting 20-30 minutes were recommended.

### Second Treatment Phase (5 1/2 to 9 months CA)

At the beginning of this period Emily developed competence in sitting, and shortly thereafter she began to pull to stand. Though foot position had been normal when Emily was in a non-weight-bearing position, the stress of standing produced abnormal and asymmetrical foot postures, with the left forefoot adducted and the right ankle pronated. Emily's abnormal arm postures, which had been corrected in prone and sitting positions, also re-emerged when she was standing and were becoming more pronounced with repetition.

At this point, the use of treatment in water was modified and used intensively. Whenever weather permitted, Emily was taken daily to the baby pool at a local park. When she was placed in a standing position, waist-deep in water, her foot position corrected almost immediately; from this normal starting position, new upright activities were introduced and practiced. Emily either stood at the side of the pool, taking support with her arms, or stood in the water with hands free, receiving manual support at the hips from mother or therapist. By this method, standing, tiptoe, semi-squat and walking were introduced. By moving from deeper to shallower water, the demand placed on Emily's postural control was increased and thus was used as a means of making activities more challenging. A diving mask and snorkle were found to be very helpful in monitoring the position of submerged body parts. In addition to ambulation activities, virtually any desired arm pattern could be obtained in the water by using floating toys. Streams of water squirted from plastic containers proved effective in obtaining grasp and release movements, pronation-supination, and isolated finger movements.

On days when it was not possible to exercise outside, a modification of the pool technique was used. Emily was placed in a plastic wastebasket filled waist-high with warm water and placed in the bathtub. This was a more restrictive setting in which to practice movement, but the effect in terms of producing normal foot and leg position was the same. Equilibrium reactions at the feet, midline weight-bearing and trunk rotation could be exercised in this situation. Foot position could be observed directly. A variety of suction toys attached to the wall were used for working on arm and hand patterns while also providing entertainment.

During the second treatment phase Emily spent 30 minutes to 1 hour daily exercising in water.

## OUTCOME

At 10 months CA Emily began walking independently. The only abnormality noted was occasional adduction of the left forefoot. With passive limb movement no increased tone could be elicited. Fine motor skills were good, with fine pincer grasp present bilaterally, although the left thumb showed occasional palmar adduction.

Since Emily's mother was competent in all treatment techniques and was a good observer, regular therapy was discontinued at this point in favor of telephone contact with the mother. When re-evaluated at 14 months CA Emily's hands were normal but occasional mild left forefoot adductus was still present.

## DISCUSSION

Bly has hypothesized that many of the undesirable movement patterns seen in high-tone children result not from the primary lesion but from the child's attempts to move against gravity with an insufficient postural base.[1] With repetition, over time, a stereotypic repertoire of movement evolves and intervention becomes progressively more difficult. This author's impression is that similar phenomena can be seen in low-tone children. This view suggests that the release from gravity provided by water would offer a favorable environment for early intervention with a wide range of disabilities. Head and trunk control and limb movements can be exercised in graded fashion by altering water depth, the position of the child and the activities used. In these situations, the child would not use maladaptive patterns of superficial postural fixation but rather would experience more normal postures and movements.

With Emily, the positive effects of exercise in water were obvious and consistent. In addition, as treatment progressed, several other general trends became apparent:

1. Tone increases apparent in abnormal posture or movements were only inconsistently detectable with passive limb movements. Over time, it became more difficult to elicit clasp-knife responses.
2. Tactile and proprioceptive intervention techniques were very effective and in fact resulted in over-correction if applied too intensively. This was particularly true during the first few months of treatment.
3. Abnormal patterns which responded well to treatment in a particular position re-emerged when developmental gains were made. For example, a strongly adducted thumb was eliminated when Emily was in the prone-on-elbows position; this re-emerged when Emily was in the prone-on-hands position. It was important to reassure the parents that this did not represent deterioration.
4. The distribution of abnormal muscle tone was somewhat changeable. Though Emily had primarily left-sided involvement, periodic flexor-type phenomena appeared in the right hand and foot.

The favorable outcome described here, of course, cannot be attributed entirely to treatment in water or even to therapy per se. The high tone might have resolved spontaneously; controlled studies will be necessary to shed light on this issue. Assuming that therapy did make a difference, however, a point must be made about consistency of treatment. In this case, Emily's mother was highly invested in the treatment and took every opportunity to modify her child's environment and playthings in a favorable direction. This, in combination with the plasticity of the child's nervous system and the mild degree of involvement, produced an ideal situation for effecting change.

## REFERENCE

1. Bly L: Abnormal motor development in Slaten DS (ed): *Development of Movement in Infancy*. University of North Carolina at Chapel Hill, 1980.

# Therapeutic Pool Activities for Young Children in a Community Facility

Karen Martin, RPT

**ABSTRACT.** With the availability of therapy pools in many communities, therapeutic pool activities and swimming can be utilized as a valuable adjunct to a regular therapy program. Although pediatric therapists have many skills with which to consult to an ongoing recreational oriented program, they need certain aquatic training and experience to initiate and supervise a therapy oriented pool program. Pool activities incorporate therapy goals and techniques for neuromuscular and orthopedic disabilities. The parent involvement and use of community resources are beneficial outcomes of the program. In addition, the psychological and physical well-being of each child develops as the experience becomes a therapeutic recreation. This article describes a four-year program and presents the rationale for a cooperative pool facility/developmental center program for young preschool children.

## INTRODUCTION

Young children with suspected or known developmental disabilities are increasingly referred to infant centers for assessment and therapy intervention. These children may be infants (under 12 months), toddlers (1-2 years of age), or preschoolers (3-6 years of age). The age of referral to therapy depends on the type of disability, the onset, and the need for intervention. In an outpatient pediatric setting, a physical therapist treats mainly young children with neuromuscular and related disabilities including cerebral palsy, muscular dystrophy, myelodysplasia, developmental delay, congenital birth anomalies, brachial plexus birth injuries, and juvenile rheumatoid arthritis. Various neurophysiological techniques and therapeutic exercises are utilized depending on the training of the therapist and the type of facility and equipment available.

Hydrotherapy has been a modality of physical therapy for many years and has been utilized by many therapists for treatment of such disabilities

---

Ms. Martin was Staff Physical Therapist, Mary Bridge Children's Health Center, Tacoma, WA, when this article was written. She is now an Itinerant Physical Therapist, Tacoma Public Schools, Tacoma, WA 98405. Her mailing address is 121 Del Monte Avenue, Tacoma, WA 98466.

as orthopedic conditions, amputations, polio, and arthritis. The size of equipment has varied from the small hand whirlpools to Hubbard tanks to actual indoor pools in hospitals and rehabilitation centers.[1] Nowadays there seems to be an ever-increasing number of health and fitness centers with large therapy pools. Even some schools for the handicapped have such pools, making therapeutic pool activities and teaching of swimming more possible than previously.[2]

The purpose of this article is to: 1) delineate the necessary components of a therapy pool program, 2) indicate the common pediatric disabilities with their therapeutic pool goals, 3) explain the preparation and administration of a therapy pool program at a community facility, and finally 4) present the potential long and short-term benefits, including parent involvement.

## COMPONENTS OF PRESCHOOL AQUATIC PROGRAM

As with any program, the components of people, facility and cooperation are necessary. Specifically for a pool program, the following are needed:

1. a pediatric physical therapist who has a swimming interest and expertise,
2. a community facility with appropriate pools and cooperative staff, and
3. a cooperative parent or caregiver with a disabled child who can benefit from therapeutic pool activities.

Having these basic components allows the therapist to consider this adjunct to the regular therapy program.

### Pediatric Physical Therapist

A pediatric physical therapist has extensive knowledge and training regarding anatomy, kinesiology, neurology, and basic components of movement. Treatment techniques include developmental therapy, therapeutic exercise and modalities, mobility and gait training, and respiratory physical therapy. Some swimming ability and aquatic training of the therapist are considered prerequisites to establishing a therapy pool program by this author. Being comfortable in and around the water is as basic as knowing water safety and life-saving procedures. With background and experience in teaching water safety and swimming, a therapist can readily adapt therapy goals to therapeutic pool activities or swimming skills. In addition, knowledge of swim instruction and progression of various strokes allows the therapist to utilize what is best for the individual child. If a therapist needs more information, usually courses are offered sometime during the summer by a local qualified water instructor of the American Red Cross or the Y.M.C.A. Aquatic staff. In fact, personnel supervising children in the water are usually required to have a current life-saving certificate. A therapist can also simply work closely with a swim instructor in order to incorporate swim skills with therapeutic pool activities. This author has found the latter a very rewarding and productive sharing of ideas.

## Pools and Equipment

Some children's hospitals, rehabilitation units and regional developmental centers do not have their own therapy pool. Within the surrounding community, however, a health fitness center or Y.M.C.A. which does have a *swimming pool* as well as a *therapy pool* is often available. With the thrust toward wheelchair accessibility, especially during the Year of the Disabled, more and more facilities are accepting and accommodating the handicapped. Such a pool facility ideally is within the local area so time and transportation are not problems. If a large *swimming pool* (10-25 meters long) is available, strokes and actual swimming skills can be emphasized for appropriate disabilities to increase endurance, strength, and range of motion. Some facilities will raise the temperature (80-84 °F) of the swimming pool for one day to accommodate a special program, while others maintain the heated (96-98 °F) therapy pool daily. Young children may or may not be very active in the water because of their disability. Warm water temperature encourages comfort, relaxation, and easier movement especially for the child with spastic cerebral palsy. The ideal situation is if the heated therapy pool is separated from the other pools and enclosed to maintain the warmth in the air.

Various commercial and homemade equipment is utilized in aquatic programs. Kick boards, swim fins, and small floatation devices can be used for effectively strengthening certain limbs while supporting part of the body. Light weight blue mats, adapted life jackets, and inflatable cuffs are common equipment used by the swimmers as well as squeeze toys, rings, sponges, and overhead mobiles. In this author's experience, the facility purchased some of the equipment and donation from a benefactor provided additional therapy balls, bolsters, folding mat, and wooden stools.

If the pools have some variation in depth a greater variety of therapeutic activities are possible. Having *stairs* for entry and exit provides opportunity for stair climbing, for sitting on steps with decreasing amounts of water support, for climbing onto the top step using leg separation and motor planning, and for possible independent entry and exit from the pool. In most cases the pool is 3-5 feet deep and young preschoolers are unable to stand on the bottom. A *platform* might be used to provide a shallow section for sitting, standing, knee walking, crab walking, and other such pool activities routinely done by all children as they experience water adjustment. The warm therapy pool ideally should vary from 1-2 feet at the shallow end to about 4 feet at the deep end.[3] Various developmental skills and facilitation can be performed in the warmest pool having a wide ledge or shallow area. The *jets* (jacuzzi) of water can be adjusted or even completely turned off to reduce the turbulence in the pool. *Deck Space* is important for changing, maneuverability, necessary equipment, and a possible treatment area.

### Parent/Caregiver

In early intervention therapy programs for infants and young children, the *parent or major caregiver* is considered an integral part of the transdisciplinary team.[4, 5] The adjunct of therapeutic pool activities is an additional commitment for the parent involving time, transportation and participation. The disabled child is usually in need of the services offered by a variety of specialists; yet the number of supplementary caregivers must be limited in order to foster a familiar and trusting relationship critical to the child's development. This transdisciplinary approach involves providing the necessary services, with one or two primary persons providing the comprehensive instruction to the caregiver.[6] With the physically disabled infant, the pediatric physical or occupational therapist often becomes that major professional worker. A positive relationship between the child and his parent must be established if the parent is to be a primary programmer. Pool therapy seems to be an avenue for developing this relationship. With each therapy session, the caregiver learns the appropriate handling and positioning techniques, as well as facilitation of voluntary normal movement patterns. Depending on the disability, specific instructions are given to the caregiver by the therapist for incorporation into the home routine. In some cases, periodic range of motion with gentle stretching is recommended and can easily be done in a therapy pool program as well as positioning, assisted movements and facilitation techniques once learned. These caregivers are learning to use their hands both effectively and economically for the benefit of their child.[7]

Long-term physical therapy of the physically disabled child is a joint therapist-parent responsibility. The family has to make special concessions and arrangements to provide this necessary care for their "special" child. Therapy intervention needs to be planned with realistic considerations of what is possible in each particular family situation.[8, 9] The adjunct of a therapy pool program can and should be scheduled without adding undue stress and commitment to the whole family. Since therapeutic pool activities are a part of the therapy intervention, they are considered therapy treatment sessions. To schedule one to two sessions at the developmental center and one session at the pool facility is feasible.

Therapy techniques learned by the parent are similar whether on land or in the water. These parents are usually cooperative and caring people who manage to balance somehow the various family commitments to include necessary therapy and to utilize recommended therapeutic techniques whenever possible. The pool therapy can be a pleasant opportunity to combine therapy, family togetherness, and some play. In fact, this author has experienced better attendance at the pool session than at the regular therapy session at the developmental center. Parents seem eager to observe, learn, and eventually attempt these specific therapeutic pool activities. The parent-child relationship seems to develop more easily in the recreational setting than the hospital setting and the child usually is more compliant with therapeutic endeavors.

This pool program begins as individual therapy and can continue as such, or possibly can become a therapeutic-based recreation for the child and his family. For the child whose life is somewhat restricted physically, pool therapy can provide a sense of freedom and relaxation. It becomes an opportunity for comfort and even play, which is considered a main road to a child's socialization.[10] Therapy has always involved a certain amount of play. This relaxing setting with increased parental involvement motivates cooperation and satisfaction for all. In some cases this pool program becomes a family recreation time with one parent in the therapy pool with the disabled child, and the other parent swimming with the other children.

## INDICATIONS AND GOALS FOR POOL PROGRAM

The reasons to begin a therapy pool program are to provide an adjunct to a regular therapy program, to increase therapeutic intervention, to increase parent involvement and to utilize available community resources. Such a program incorporates the therapy goals specific to each individual and his disability as indicated. Pool therapy allows for diversity in approach and increased cooperation. In fact, therapeutic aquatics are a way of developing a therapeutic based and beneficial recreation for the child and his family.

Basic criteria for initiation of this therapeutic pool approach are: 1) the disability would benefit by pool therapy, 2) the child must be between the ages of 4 months and 6 years (which is the age range serviced by the developmental center and infants under 4 months are not allowed in public facility pools); 3) the child must have a current medical health clearance from a primary physician in addition to center-based therapy referral; and 4) the parents must make a commitment involving transportation, active participation in the pool, and willingness to utilize the pool on their own once trained.

As the families of pool program participants mingle with each other, exposure to the reality of children with disabilities is increased. The parents and children become accustomed to looks and questions and, in turn, develop their own way of responding. Such an experience is vital to ongoing acceptance and involvement in the community. This exposure is mainstreaming in recreation which, hopefully, can be a part of everyone's life.

As the child develops an ability to move and enjoy the water, he seems to improve his self-awareness and his inner self-esteem. The achievement of simple skills or moving on his own allows for a beginning sense of independence and accomplishment.

Persons with certain neuromuscular and orthopedic disabilities, more than others, can benefit from therapeutic pool activities. Joints which are difficult to move or have limited motion are often easier to move in the water, as is beginning movement when it has been restricted or abnormal. Therapy goals and therapy pool activities for some disabilities will be discussed, based on the author's personal experience.

### Children with Muscular Dystrophy, Juvenile Rheumatoid Arthritis, and Congenital Anomalies

Children with *muscular dystrophy, juvenile rheumatoid arthritis*, and *congenital birth anomalies* have limited range of motion, limited active movement, strong tendency to develop contractures or deformities, limited functional mobility skills, insufficient respiratory function, and discomfort or pain in muscles and joints. Physical therapy intervention attempts to relieve the discomfort, to maintain or increase the active movements of all joints, to prevent the deformities, and to increase the respiratory status. The overall therapy for these goals includes passive and active range of motion, which effectively can be done in a warm therapy pool. The child can either sit in the pool (if shallow enough), hold onto the side, or wear a life preserver to keep him afloat while the therapist assists with the joint movements. Furthermore, the warmth of the water relaxes the muscles, making the child more comfortable and the joints easier to move.

Non-weight bearing active exercises are beneficial for arthritic or muscular conditions.[11] A child holding a kick board with out-stretched arms in maximum shoulder flexion while she kicks her feet to move forward in the water allows some stretching of tight shoulder flexors and hip flexors (Figure 1). This is one example of a swimming skill used for a child with joint limitations from congenital birth anomalies. As the child can tolerate and improve his prone position, he can increase his range of motion and his strength by kicking greater distances. Climbing in and out of the pool can increase mobility and strength of arms, legs, and trunk.

FIGURE 1. A child with congenital birth anomalies doing active stretching.

Blowing bubbles, holding a breath under water for longer periods, and breathing through the nose with mouth closed all increase respiratory function, as well as oral motor control.

These activities are beginning swim skills, which once learned, can progress to the child swimming in some manner actively on his own. A child might use a small foam belt to achieve needed body position to swim a simple elementary back stroke (Figure 2). Each child is challenged to be as independent as possible. With the muscle weakness of muscular dystrophy, floating and swimming on the back seems the easiest and safest, yet these children must also learn a recovery method, like rolling to one side and holding the edge of the pool. They need the buoyancy of the water in order to perform such skills as jumping, hopping, climbing up a larger step, or knee walking. The excitement and thrill of a child finally performing a skill independently is extremely rewarding.

### Children with Mild Cerebral Palsy

Children with mild *cerebral palsy*, spastic diplegia, have abnormal muscle tone and abnormal movement patterns which limit mobility skills. Using neurodevelopmental techniques to obtain a more normal postural tone involves proper handling and positioning. By providing some assistance to inhibit abnormal reflex activity, the child may be facilitated into more normal movements.[7] Neurodevelopmental Techniques (NDT) emphasizing pelvic mobility, leg dissociation, and trunk rotation done in a warm therapy pool (36°C-38°C or 96°F-100°F) help relieve the hypertonus in the child with spastic cerebral palsy. Combining total immersion in warm water with proper handling enhances the treatment technique and the benefit for the child.[2] Initially, total immersion with minimal active movement for a period of 15-20 minutes reduces the effect of spasticity. Then a therapist can facilitate specific movements in the pool or on a nearby mat. A two-year old may be able to sit on a small step in the pool with minimal hand support and graduate to no hand support needed. The child may be able to get heels down more readily and attempt coming to standing with minimal assistance. The child with mild spastic diplegia may be able to assume and maintain half-kneeling transition to standing since the water serves as a medium providing support (Figure 3). This same support factor makes it more possible for a young child to walk first in the water prior to achieving such a skill on land.

### Children with Severe Quadriplegic Involvement

Certain young children with *severe quadriplegic involvement* have fluctuating tone or increased spasticity often making even passive movements of the limbs difficult. Gradual total immersion in warm water for relief of the hypertonus allows gentle movement through the maximal range of

FIGURE 2. A child swimming a simple elementary back stroke wearing foam belt.

FIGURE 3. A child with spastic diplegia doing half-kneeling transition.

each joint, and is imperative to prevent increased tightness and limitation of passive movement. Maintaining range of motion of all joints is necessary in order to provide proper hygiene; to be able to dress the child; and even to allow for proper positioning to prevent skin breakdown or pressure sores. If the child is healthy enough to be an outpatient for therapy, probably he is able to use the therapy pool rather than a Hubbard tank. Although the child's physical activity is limited, the parent and therapist can easily exercise his limbs and trunk in a therapy pool. Exercise is accomplished by some person holding the child while the other rotates the pelvis or moves the limbs. Adapted or special life jackets can be used to support the child in a back-float position, allowing freer movement.

### Children with Brachial Plexus Birth Injury

Brachial plexus birth injury is most commonly unilateral and involves temporary paralysis of the muscles innervated by specific cervical nerve roots. Initially a pediatric therapist and parent maintain the range of motion. The therapy pool is an ideal setting to provide sensory stimulation and facilitate some active movement, once the infant is old enough to be in a public pool. The youngest age permitted by the pool facility for this author was 4 months old. Therapy intervention in most cases began at one or two days of age with passive movements and positioning by the parents and active water activities during bath time at home. Being in a pool allows more room for spontaneous paddling of the arms and kicking of the legs. Simple activities like splashing, pushing bubbles and reaching are easier because of the buoyancy of the water. The parent can sit in the shallow area holding the infant in different ways so as to facilitate increased arm movements. The warm water helps to keep the infant warm and comfortable for the short period of time. The pool program lasts about 20-30 minutes, depending on the amount of total immersion, the exact temperature of the water that day, and the tolerance of the child. Each child's tolerance is different and can be easily judged by behavior, activity level, and flushing of the child's cheeks.

## PLANNING AND PROMOTION OF POOL PROGRAM

Establishing a therapy pool program is a cooperative effort by the therapist, developmental center, the facility and the family. All of those involved are making a commitment of time and energy. The initial contact and the arrangements for a therapy-related program are shared by the therapist and the administrations of both facilities.

## Proposal

For the described program, a proposal was submitted to the department head for approval by the developmental center. Once approved, it was submitted to the aquatic director of the pool facility. The physical therapist, as program coordinator, actually prepared and presented the proposal to both administrations. The proposal included the purpose of the program, the arrangements, the benefits of a pool program, and a request for a six-month trial period. This specific pool program was designed to provide an adjunct to a regular therapy program allowing for diversity in approach and techniques.

## Arrangements

As an introduction, small informal presentations were held by the therapist for the staff and members of the fitness center. In addition, an article appeared in the monthly newsletter. These two procedures seemed to facilitate acceptance by those fitness center members who were sometimes inconvenienced by fussing, yelling, or crowding in the therapy pool or dressing rooms.

The families visited the facility and were informed about the rules and regulations prior to the initiation of the program. Pool facilities have such rules as:

1. cloth diaper must be worn under bathing suit for infants;
2. dressing is done only in dressing rooms;
3. special cards are to be used at front desk for admission; and
4. everyone must take a complete shower before entering the pool.

Prior information reduces the number of mishaps or complaints. One person may be the liaison between therapist and the pool facility, to improve and facilitate both communication and organization. A specific contact person helps to clarify schedules and to transfer messages. Occasionally unexpected cancellations occur because of pool malfunctions, illness, or transportation problems. In this program the contact person has been a physical education professional/aquatic coordinator with a special interest in adapted aquatics.

## Benefits

Working in a different medium (water) provides a challenge to the therapist and an opportunity for increased therapy intervention with increased parent involvement. Often during center-based therapy sessions the caregiver tended to watch and converse with the therapist rather than actively participate, whereas, during the pool therapy, once the parent is wet and in the water, he readily becomes involved in the therapeutic pool activities. The therapy treatment seems to be more effective for the child is usually more cooperative and the parent is physically involved. The parents have indicated that the child is easier to handle or is able to move actively on his own with less restriction for one to two hours following pool therapy. This factor alone seems to encourage consistent attendance by the families. As the child attempts difficult skills and enjoys freer movement, he seems to feel better about himself.

Fortunately the pool facility was already servicing some disabled clients and the staff seemed eager to incorporate another special program. This program was serving an age range that currently was not being served. No plans were being made for a therapy pool as part of the rehabilitation unit within the near future and this therapist felt use should be made of presently available community resources. Furthermore, a need always exists for facilities and people to accommodate the disabled more readily. Families with a disabled child need places in the community that are accessible and accepting. Activities and recreation are necessary parts of our lives. This cooperative venture seemed to have benefits for all concerned.

## Funding

The developmental center was eager to expand services if the cost effectiveness could be maintained. Therapeutic pool activities are physical therapy and were billed as such. Reimbursement for transportation was arranged for the therapist. No financial charge was made for use of the pool facility since the therapy sessions did not interrupt scheduled aquatic programming.

Use of facilities at a fitness center often require a membership fee or monthly dues, which may or may not be financially feasible for families of disabled children. If the family cannot afford the fee, special scholarships can be arranged through the facility or through community funding groups with only a minimal charge to the family, if any. Each child becomes a junior member for the six months and the parent is considered a volunteer at no extra charge. In fact, membership permitted the families to come at other times during the week once the program was established.

## Review of Program

After three months a review of the program was done to improve accountability. Eight children, ranging in ages from 12 months to 3.6 years were enrolled in the six month trial period. Therapy attendance was 85%, with twelve out of fourteen scheduled visits made each week. Five of the children appeared eager to come to the pool, and indeed encouraged parents to bring them. The other three children were too involved or too young to communicate a desire to come to the pool. As mentioned previously, the parents seemed motivated by observable benefits to continue this pool therapy. Subjectively, this therapist felt tone changes, making facilitation of movements easier. Changes in tone resulting from pool therapy might be an area for future research, using a more objective method. Certain children could actually move more freely and completely, providing themselves with their own positive feedback. At the end of six months, the attendance had fluctuated, going as low at 75% (eleven out of fourteen visits); however, this was during the winter and two families were having transportation difficulties. Overall, the goals of the program were being met, and the staff decided to continue the program. In fact this cooperative pool therapy program has continued over four years with the same pool facility.

## INDIVIDUALIZED PROGRAM AND CURRICULUM

### Individualized program

As indicated previously, this aquatic approach is an adjunct to therapy, and structured to achieve therapy goals. Many pediatric therapists routinely write therapy long-term goals (annual) and some short-term objectives (quarterly) which might be referred to as part of an Individualized Educational Program (IEP). A physical therapy goal might be for child to maintain or improve a certain range of motion. Therapeutic pool activities provide ideal opportunities for objectives to be achieved by the child.[12] The specifics of each objective depend on the disability, the amount of involvement and the functional level of the child. For example—J. will flutter kick on front, holding the kick board with straight arms 10 lengths of pool (10 yards). Depending on the therapy goal, the number of lengths can be increased or a time factor included.

### Water Adjustment

In most cases a period of water adjustment, involving watching, sitting in the water, and, hopefully, beginning water play is needed.[13] This first exposure to the pool needs to be enjoyable, yet beneficial to the child. Enough time must be allotted for a gradual introduction, especially if the child shows any sign of apprehension or fear. As the toddler or preschooler becomes more familiar with the setting, the people and the water, more can be accomplished.

## Safety

Safety procedures and skills are a very important part of each child's curriculum. Specific safety rules are explained by the lifeguard to the parents as part of their training and to the children who are able to comprehend. For example:

1. anyone entering a pool must shower;
2. only walking is allowed on deck; or
3. the lifeguard is the person in charge in the pool area.

As the children progress in abilities, procedures such as use of life jackets and ring buoy are taught when appropriate.

## Mainstreaming

Three of the youngsters were gradually integrated into toddler-parent swim classes with therapist consultation to the swim instructors. These children were mildly involved and were either able to perform most of the water activities taught or readily adapted their own method.

## Special Curriculum

The more physically disabled preschoolers initially had pool therapy and gradually learned the swimming skills of a special curriculum used by the adapted aquatics program at the pool facility. This curriculum, Swimming With Integrated Movement, has been developed by Alice Walter, pediatric physical therapist, and Marilee Fijalka-Carr, adapted aquatics coordinator, for children with severe and profound handicaps to children who are mainstreamed. Each of the various program areas (safety, breathing, buoyancy and body position, and body movements) are broken down into small steps of achievement which are therapeutically based. For example: A child is credited (a check or star) for eye contact, head held in midline, or holding breath for 3 seconds. Accomplishing certain skills allows the child to earn a rating of a special kind of fish. Certain levels are applicable to young preschoolers as well as older school-aged youngsters.

## SUMMARY

Therapeutic pool activities for young children in a community facility are an additional experience that some developmental therapy centers can provide for handicapped children. With the availability of a therapy pool and adequately trained therapists, a pool program can become a beneficial adjunct to a regular therapy program. Enthusiastic parent involvement has been one of the most valuable assets. The information shared in this article is intended to encourage fellow pediatric therapists to consider aquatics an adjunct to therapy, to consider further research regarding changes in muscle tone during pool therapy and to consider the short and long term psychological effects of a pool therapy program on the child and his family.

## REFERENCES

1. Stewart J: Exercises in water. In Licht (ed): *Therapeutic Exercise*, ed 2. Baltimore, Waverly Press, 1956, pp 285-295.

2. Harris S: Neurodevelopmental treatment approach for teaching swimming to cerebral palsied children. *Phys Ther* 58: 979-983, 1978.

3. Williams CE: Physical therapy in residential facilities. In Pearson PR, Williams CE (eds): *Physical Therapy Services in the Developmental Disabilities*, ed 6. Springfield, IL, Charles C Thomas, 1978, pp 457-458.

4. Sparling J: The transdisciplinary approach with the developmentally delayed child. *Phys & Occ Ther in Pediatrics* 1: 3-13, 1980.

5. Connor FP, Williamson GG, Siepp JM: *Program Guide for Infants and Toddlers With Neuromotor and Other Developmental Disabilities*. New York, Teachers College Press, 1978.

6. Brown SL, Moersch MS: *Parents On The Team*. Ann Arbor, The University of Michigan Press, 1982.

7. Finnie, NR: *Handling The Young Cerebral Palsied Child at Home*, ed 2. New York, EP Dutton and Co, 1975, pp 51-67, 82-90.

8. Fieber N, Kliewer D: Physical therapy in a children's rehabilitation center. In Pearson PH, Williams CE (eds): *Physical Therapy Services in the Developmental Disabilities*, ed 6. Springfield, IL, Charles C Thomas, 1978, pp 404-406.

9. Lucca JA, Settler BH: Effects of children's disabilities on parental time use, *Phys Ther* 61: 196-201, 1981.

10. Spock B, Lerrigo MO: *Caring for Your Disabled Child*. New York, The MacMillan Co, 1968, pp 195-220.

11. Miller JJ: Juvenile rheumatoid arthritis. In Bleck EE, Nagel DA (eds): *Physically Handicapped Children: A Medical Atlas for Teachers*. New York, Grune & Stratton, 1975, pp 233-239.

12. Dulcy F: Essential considerations for an integrated, developmental aquatic program model for school-aged disabled children. Thesis, Emory University, 1981.

13. Reynolds G: *A Swimming Program for the Handicapped*. New York, Associated Press, (National Board of Young Men's Christian Association), 1973 pp 25, 29.

# Water as a Learning Environment
# for Facilitating Gross Motor Skills
# in Deaf-Blind Children

Susan R. Harris, PhD, RPT
Marie Thompson, PhD

**ABSTRACT.** An overview of a specialized pool program for deaf-blind children is presented in which the goal is to facilitate the achievement of gross motor, social and communication skills in a water environment, with subsequent generalization of these skills to other settings. The gross motor portion of this project is described including a case study of a deaf-blind youngster who participated in this program. The case study includes a detailed description of the long-term gross motor goals and short-term objectives which were developed for him as part of the project. Progress toward achievement of these objectives is depicted on both a data recording sheet and a graph.

Specialized pool therapy or swimming programs have been recommended for children with a variety of handicapping conditions including children with cerebral palsy,[1] mental retardation,[2] learning disabilities,[3] muscular dystrophy,[4] hemophilia,[5] cystic fibrosis,[6] and meningomyelocele.[7] Goals of these various programs have included the reduction of spasticity and inhibition of tonic reflex patterns,[1] the promotion of socialization and peer interaction,[3] and the maintenance or improvement of pulmonary function.[4, 6]

In November, 1980, a unique model swimming program was initiated for a group of severely handicapped deaf-blind children who are residents of a state institution in Washington. The primary goal of this program was to use the water as a learning environment for the achievement of gross motor, social and communication skills among these children with multi-

Susan R. Harris is Assistant Professor, Division of Physical Therapy, Department of Rehabilitation Medicine RJ-30, University of Washington, Seattle, WA 98195. Marie Thompson is Assistant Professor, Area of Special Education, College of Education, University of Washington.

This study was supported by Contract No. 300-80-0645, Integrated Educational/Leisure Time Model for Deaf-Blind Children and Youth, from the United States Department of Education, Special Education Programs, to the University of Washington, College of Education (Marie Thompson, PhD, Principal Investigator). The opinions expressed herein do not necessarily reflect the position or the policy of the United States Department of Education and no official endorsement by the United States Department of Education should be inferred.

ple sensory and motor impairments. Secondary goals included the generalization of these skills to other environments such as a gymnasium setting, the classroom, and living settings. The ultimate long-term goal of this program was to enable these children, through the achievement of functional gross motor, social, and communication skills, to move out of the institution and into less sheltered living settings such as group homes or semi-independent living sites.

The purpose of this article is to describe the use of the water environment as a medium for the facilitation of developmental and functional gross motor skills. As the project's physical therapist during the first year of this three-year model demonstration program, the senior author was responsible for developing specific gross motor objectives for each child which could be carried out in the swimming pool and then generalized into the gymnasium, classroom and living settings.

## ASSESSMENT PROCEDURES

### Subjects

Seventeen deaf-blind children were initially assessed during the first year of the project. Participants ranged in age from 4 to 19 years. All but the youngest child, who lived with her family, were residents of the institution; all attended school at the institution. In addition to their visual and auditory impairments, all of the children were functioning in the severely and profoundly retarded ranges. Fourteen of the children also had been diagnosed as having cerebral palsy. Other handicapping conditions which were present in a number of children included seizure disorders, fixed orthopedic deformities, and bowel and bladder incontinence.

### Assessment Tools

Each child was assessed by a team to measure social, communication and gross motor skills. In order to generate appropriate gross motor objectives, all children were assessed using three developmental instruments; the Bayley Scales of Infant Development;[8] the Callier-Azusa Scale for deaf-blind children,[9] and the Fircrest Deaf-Blind Motor Assessment Tool.[10]

To illustrate how the assessment data were used in developing specific gross motor objectives to be carried out in the swimming pool and other environments, a case study of one of the children is presented in the following section. This child's progress toward the achievement of those objectives is also discussed and presented on a graph.

## CASE STUDY

Rick is a deaf-blind youngster who was 11 years 2 months of age when he was initially assessed in November 1980. The etiology of his combined visual and auditory impairments is unknown although probably prenatal, according to his hospital records. He was a premature twin, delivered at 34 weeks gestation by emergency Caesarean section. The other twin died at 72 hours of age. Rick was on a respirator for 4 days because of prolonged anoxia and idiopathic respiratory distress syndrome. Currently, Rick is functioning in the severely retarded range, has no vision, and has a moderate to severe hearing loss. He is enrolled in a classroom of children who are also classified as severely to profoundly retarded and who have either vision, hearing, or combined vision and hearing impairments.

In all skill areas assessed—gross motor, communication, and social—Rick was the highest functioning child in our group of 17 children. He was capable of combining two-word signs in expressive communication and could also respond to two-word signed commands. With prompts, he was independent in dressing and undressing except for shoe-tying. He was semi-independent in toileting but had occasional incidents of urinary and fecal incontinence during the early phases of the project.

On the Bayley Motor Scale, Rick achieved a developmental age equivalent score of 24 months. He was able to rise to standing and walk independently. He could jump in place with feet together, walk on tiptoes, and attempt a step on the balance board. He could walk up and down stairs, with support, using a marked-time stepping pattern but was unable to walk up or down stairs without some outside support. On the *Postural Control* subscale of the Callier-Azusa Scale, Rick passed all items through 22 months with scattered passes through 60 months. His highest pass was the ability to stand up from the floor without hand support (60 months on Callier-Azusa). On the *Locomotion* subscale, he passed all items through 18 months with scattered passes through 36 months (pedaling and steering a tricycle). On the Fircrest Deaf-Blind Motor Assessment Tool, Rick received an age equivalent score of 26 months. Automatic reactions present included hopping reactions sideways, forward, and backward.[12] Dorsiflexion equilibrium reactions were present inconsistently and were thus scored as a failure.

Based on this initial assessment information, two long-term gross motor goals were developed for Rick: 1) to increase independence in functional mobility skills, and 2) to improve balance in standing. Specific short-term objectives were developed for each of these goals. Every effort was made to develop objectives that were both developmentally and functionally appropriate.

Since one of Rick's earliest failures developmentally was the inability to ascend and descend stairs without hand support, these activities were selected as objectives which would be both developmentally and functionally relevant. Functional relevance stemmed from the feeling that Rick might one day be in a situation in the community where he would need to ascend or descend stairs without outside hand support. Since Rick's current mode of ascending and descending stairs *with* hand support was to use a "marked-time" gait (always leading with the same foot), the initial short-term objectives specified that he could use this pattern (see Figure 1). Once Rick achieved criterion using a marked-time stepping pattern, subsequent objectives would specify the use of alternating stepping patterns—first for ascending and then for descending since this is the sequence in which a normal child learns these behaviors.

Since the buoyancy of water provides a supportive environment for performing functional skills such as standing, walking, and stair climbing[1] and thus minimizes the need for independent balance, Rick's activities were first conducted on the bottom three steps of the broad stairs leading into the pool, thus allowing the water to provide support for the lower trunk and lower extremities. The first two short-term objectives, therefore, were: 1) Rick will *ascend* the bottom 3 steps in the pool (marking time) without hand support, for 3 consecutive data days, and 2) Rick will *descend* the bottom 3 steps in the pool (marking time) without hand support, for 3 consecutive data days. The antecedent cues for each of these objectives were combined loud verbal and signed cues to "Step up, Rick!" and "Step down, Rick!"

Data were recorded daily by project staff on both objectives (Figure 1) and then were subsequently graphed (Figure 2). Criterion was achieved if Rick successfully ascended and descended all three steps without hand support or other outside assist. If he successfully ascended and descended more than 3 steps, he was given credit for the number of steps both on the data sheet and on the graph (Figures 1 and 2). Since an alternating stepping gait is developmentally more advanced than marked-time stepping, Rick was not penalized for alternated stepping even though the objective specified marked-time stepping. The consequence for successful behavior was appropriate praise, both verbal and signed, i.e., "Good stepping up, Rick!" with a pat on the head. The consequence for unsuccessful behavior was a firm verbal and signed, "No, Rick!" followed by a repeat trial with physical prompting underneath the popliteal space. As can be seen from the graphed objectives (Figure 2), Rick consistently achieved the ascending objective from the very start of the program but consistency to criterion (3 days) for the descending objective took 7 data days over a period of 2 1/2 weeks.

The gross motor, social, and communication objectives were carried out in the pool during 30-minute sessions on the first four days of each week. On Fridays, objectives were carried out in a gymnasium setting

Figure 1: Data Sheet for Objectives

DAILY DATA SHEET FOR ____Gross Motor____ SKILLS

STUDENT'S NAME: ____Rick____

OBJECTIVE: 1) Rick will ascend the bottom 3 steps in the pool (marking time) without hand support, for 3 consecutive data days. 2) Rick will descend the bottom 3 steps in the pool (marking time) without hand support, for 3 consecutive data days.

| DATE | ASCENDING STAIRS | | | | DESCENDING STAIRS | | | COMMENTS: |
|------|---|---|---|---|---|---|---|---|
| 1-7-81 | + | + | + | | - | + | + | |
| 1-8-81 | + | + | + | | + | + | + | Criterion #1 achieved. |
| 1-12-81 | + | + | + | | + | + | + | Criterion #2 achieved. |
| 1-14-81 | + | + | + | | - | - | - | Held onto railing during descending. |
| 1-19-81 | + | + | + | | + | + | + | Criterion #1 achieved. |
| 1-21-81 | + | + | + | | + | + | + | Criterion #2 achieved. |
| 1-27-81 | + | + | + | | + | + | + | Criterion #3 achieved. |

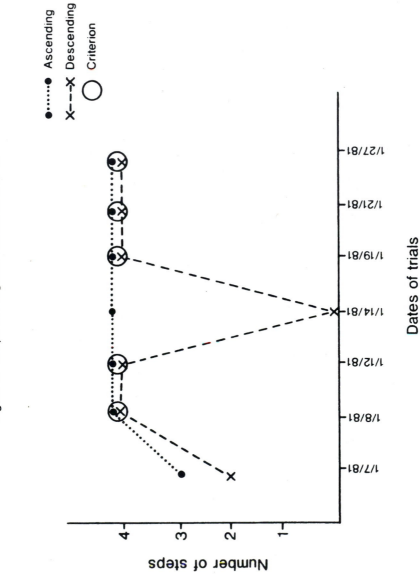

Figure 2: Graph of Progress Toward Objectives

with the goal of generalizing these behaviors to "dry land." Rick's objectives on the gymnasium steps were exactly the same as those in the pool except that he lacked the supportive benefit of the water medium. Rick quickly generalized his newly-acquired pool skills to the non-water setting. His classroom teachers and the staff in the residence building where he lived were also instructed in methods for carrying out the objectives, thus providing further generalization of these skills.

## CONCLUSIONS

The use of a pool setting to initiate functional and developmentally-appropriate gross motor skills in children with severe multiple handicaps can be a valuable adjunct to more traditional therapy approaches. A water environment provides opportunities to utilize varying degrees of support for children with inadequate balance skills as well as providing opportunities for freedom of movement, the experience of buoyancy or weight-relief, and vestibular stimulation. The psychological benefits of successful achievement, with concomitant rewards provided by the trainers, is an equally valuable reason for using such a setting.

With severely handicapped children, such as those involved in our program, therapists must be able to develop measurable, behavioral objectives which are further delineated into small sequential steps in order to document progress as a result of their intervention.[11] We feel that the benefits of a pool environment combined with our precision in developing specific, quantifiable objectives contributed to the success of Rick and other children in the program in achieving measurable gains in gross motor, social, and communication skills.

## REFERENCES

1. Harris SR: Neurodevelopmental treatment approach for teaching swimming to cerebral palsied children. *Phys Ther* 58:979-983, 1978.
2. Bundschuh EL, Williams EW, Hollingworth JD: Teaching the retarded to swim. *Ment Retard* 10: 14-17, 1972.
3. Martino L, Johnson DW: Comparative and individualistic experiences among disabled and normal children. *J Soc Psychol* 107:177-183, 1979.
4. Chandler LS, Adams MA: Effects of physical therapy program on vital capacity of patients with muscular dystrophy. *Phys Ther* 54: 494-496, 1974.
5. Andonian AA, Dietrich SL, Whiteman ST: A total program for the patient with hemophilia. *J Am Phys Ther Assn* 46: 1268-1285, 1966.
6. Clement M, Jankowski LW, Beaudry PH: Prone immersion physical exercise therapy in three children with cystic fibrosis: A pilot study. *Nurs Res* 28: 325-328, 1979.
7. Dowrick PW, Dove C: The use of self-modeling to improve the swimming performance of spina bifida children. *J App Beh Anal* 13: 51-56, 1980.
8. Bayley N: *The Bayley Scales of Infant Development* New York, Psychological Corporation, 1969.
9. Stillman R (ed): *The Callier-Azusa Scale.* Dallas, Callier Center for Communication Disorders, University of Texas, 1977.
10. Harris SR: *Fircrest Deaf-Blind Motor Assessment Tool.* Unpublished assessment tool, 1980.

11. O'Neill DL, Harris SR: Developing goals and objectives for handicapped children. *Phys Ther* 62: 295-298, 1982.

12. Fiorentino MR: *Reflex Testing Methods for Evaluating CNS Disorders*. Springfield IL, Charles C Thomas, 1973.

# ANNOTATED BIBLIOGRAPHY

## Aquatics for Disabled Persons

Susan M. Attermeier, MACT, LPT
Faye H. Dulcy, MMSc, RPT
Susan R. Harris, PhD, RPT
Karen Martin, RPT

### GENERAL REFERENCES

Duffield MH (ed): *Exercise in Water.* New York, McMillan Publishing Co., 1976.

The existing dearth of literature on therapeutic pool programming, in addition to the completeness of this book, contribute to its being one of the most outstanding and practical references available. *Exercise in Water* is highly recommended for American physical therapy students, practicing physical therapists, and persons in other disciplines working with pool programs. According to the editor, *Exercise in Water* was written as a textbook for British student physiotherapists. The information provided is useful for planning and implementing new programs, as well as for consulting to existing programs. Both basic principles and methods upon which to build a diverse and complete program are included.

The book begins with a very complete discussion and description of the physical properties of water and their application to principles of hydrodynamics. The physiological and therapeutic effects of exercise in warm water are also discussed. Although these topics are vital to the development and understanding of effective pool programming, the thoroughness of these discussions are rewarding and unusual as few other texts seem to explore them as completely. Methods and principles for variation in activity and exercise progression based on use of changes in body position and equipment adjuncts are described in the first chapter and elaborated in later chapters.

*Exercise in Water* includes discussion of untoward effects, dangers and precautions for pool programs, methods of prevention and emergency management. Pools, tanks, and recommended accessory equipment are described. Theoretical treatment procedures for patient as well as general procedures for therapists are also detailed.

Three chapters are devoted to the treatment of specific disorders: rheumatoid, neurological, and orthopedic conditions. Pediatric treatment and use of games conclude the book.

In several places throughout the book, the point is made that swimming rather than pool therapy might be indicated for certain conditions. Although reflecting an apparent unidisciplinary "swimming or therapy" approach, this book is written in language understandable by staff with either recreational or therapeutic orientations. The only prerequisites for comprehension of the book's language appears to be the nomenclature used to describe body movements.


Grosse SJ, McGill CD: Independent swimming for children with severe physical impairments. *Practical Pointers* 3(2):1-15, 1979.

The authors stress the importance of allowing persons with severe physical handicaps to actually become independent swimmers, rather than just passive participants in a recreational experience. The first step toward independence is water adjustment. The authors outline eight steps toward the achievement of water adjustment, emphasizing the importance of communicating to the student what is going to happen to her next and allowing her the opportunity to make a "yes" or "no" response to the initiation of each subsequent phase.

Concomitant with the introduction of water adjustment is the introduction of breath control, an absolute necessity for independent swimming. Progressions in developing breath control include dunking and graduated breath holding under water. During both water adjustment and breath control activities, the child is positioned vertically with support given under the axillae by the instructor.

Mobility, the third step toward independent swimming, is introduced when the student has become comfortable in the water and can hold her breath for at least 7-8 seconds. Floating in both prone and supine positions is taught. Once independent floating is achieved in each position, mobility is superimposed. The authors stress that "any movement is acceptable" and regular swimming strokes cannot always be expected. The final phase in developing mobility is the ability to move from supine to prone and prone to supine; this phase is referred to as recovery. Final steps toward independent swimming include independence in pool entry and pool exit.

The authors conclude that independent swimming is possible for "almost any person." They stress the importance of allowing students to participate in their own goal-setting and decision-making and allowing them the opportunity to experiment.

Elkington HJ: The effective use of the pool. *Physiotherapy* 57:452-460, 1971.

The author's purpose was to encourage the imaginative use of pool activities for handicapped individuals. To this end she presents general guidelines and principles of aquatherapy. Prerequisites to successful water activity include a knowledge of the learner's background, suitable physical setting, a positive relationship between instructor and learner, and the ability of the instructor to provide constant challenge for experimentation and exploration.

Preparation for and methods of entering water are briefly discussed. Movement in water is more extensively addressed. This includes adaptive aids, principles of buoyancy, propulsion, breathing and submerging. Basic swimming patterns are described and diagrammed, as are a selection of water games using ropes and submerged equipment.

The article does not specifically address possible adaptations for different handicapping conditions. It should be helpful reading for the therapist inexperienced in aquatherapy.

Newman J: *Swimming for Children with Physical and Sensory Impairments.* Springfield, IL, Charles C Thomas, 1976.

The general theme of this book is that every child, no matter how handicapped, can be instructed in pool activities for the purposes of physical improvement, recreation and personal fulfillment. The author, a recreation education therapist, presents a general technique of "swim patterning" for teaching basic swimming strokes to handicapped children and adolescents.

The first chapter describes "swim patterning," which consists of a graded series of physically guided limb movements which lead to performance of the basic repertoire of swim strokes. Subsequent chapters describe specific adaptations of the method for the child with spina bifida, traumatic paraplegia, cerebral palsy, multiple birth defects, blindness, deafness, juvenile rheumatoid arthritis, and hydrocephalus. Throughout these chapters, breath control, independent flotation and water safety are stressed as basic skills. Two chapters are devoted to methods of organizing swim meets and shows. The final three chapters consist of questions and answers, definitions of terminology, and sample evaluation forms and lesson plans.

The author's enthusiasm for swim therapy is contagious and she offers a multitude of practical suggestions, clearly based on extensive experience. This is, however, a personal rather than a scholarly work, and is seriously flawed. The author does not exhibit in-depth understanding of handicapping conditions, particularly cerebral palsy. Dysfunction related to spasticity is often attributed to "weakness." Furthermore, the text implies that by progressing from passive to active-assistive to active movement, within the patterns described, coordinate movement can be achieved. In discussion of other disabilities, over-generalization and lack of qualification is a frequent occurrence.

Stylistically, the book is informal and "chatty," replete with self-admitted "digressions" into philosophical areas. It has no bibliography and only a minimal number of footnotes. The "terminology" list contains grossly inadequate and often inaccurate definitions (example—Stimulation: making a child able to move). Indeed, at times one gets the impression that the author spoke directly to the typesetter without the benefit of an editor.

This book can in no sense be used as a primary source of information. The knowledgeable therapist may find it of value for its practical suggestions.

Reynolds GD (ed): *A Swimming Program for the Handicapped.* New York, National YMCA, 1973.

This booklet is a manual for people working in the field of swimming for the disabled of any age. It is the result of a research project and proposals for developing and improving YMCA aquatic programs over a two-three year period in the early 1970s.

Prerequisites for establishing a swimming program are discussed, as well as the importance of recruitment and training of aquatic leaders and volunteers. Basic teaching techniques and movement exploration activities are reviewed with some innovations based on the individual's disability. Simple explanations in lay terms are given for various conditions in addition to specific suggestions for using swimming as a medium for activity.

Overall, the information is limited and needs to be updated.

Bradtke JS: *Adaptive Devices for Aquatic Activities.* American Alliance for Health, Physical Education, Recreation and Dance, 1979.

This pamphlet presents information about commercial and homemade devices used for getting into the pool and in the water. Individuals having different disabling conditions can use this equipment. Some of the devices are illustrated. Sources and addresses are listed for the commercial equipment. Selected reprints from AAHPERD and IRUC are listed with cost and source. The suggestions are helpful and stimulate even more creativity in providing beneficial aquatic experiences.

## ASTHMA

Chai H, Falliers C: Controlled swimming in asthmatic children: An evaluation of physiological and subjective data. *J Allergy* (abs) 41(2):93, 1968.

This abstract briefly describes a study conducted to assess the value of swimming as an adjunct to long-term rehabilitation of asthmatic children. Thirty subjects participated in a 12-week study. During six of those weeks the children swam for 40 minutes a day under the direction of a physical therapist. Each child received twice weekly clinical examinations and a variety of pulmonary physiology measurements were taken at daily or weekly intervals. When the control and active phases were compared no significant differences on physiological measurements were found. All children, however, reported subjective improvement.

The authors suggest that asthma should be considered a "two-component syndrome—subjective and physiological—each of which is real but not necessarily correlated with the other."

Fitch KD, Morton AR, Blanksby BA: Effects of swimming training on children with asthma. *Arch Dis Child* 51:190-194, 1976.

This study was carried out to determine the effects of regular swimming training on the otherwise unaltered lives of asthmatic school children. The subjects were 46 children aged 9 to 16 years. A pretraining evaluation consisted of a variety of medical, physiological and anthropometric measures. These included medical and exercise history; posture evaluation; and measurement of height, weight, chest circumference, chest diameter, and percentage of body fat. In addition, a challenge for exercise-induced asthma (EIA) was carried out using a treadmill; from this, physical work capacity (PWC) was calculated. Medication levels were recorded initially and monitored throughout the training period.

Following the initial assessment, the subjects received professional coaching in swimming for five months, working gradually up to 5 one-hour sessions per week. At the end of the five month period, the original measures were repeated and the subjects filled in a detailed questionnaire to elicit their subjective reactions to the program.

Findings included reduction of body fat despite increased body mass, improved posture, improved swimming ability and increased PWC. Mean medication levels decreased, though this may have been partially the result of seasonal variation in pollen counts and asthma. Exercise induced asthma showed no change. No negative side-effects were noted, and the subjective reactions of both children and parents were very positive.

The authors concluded that regular swimming training was a highly suitable form of physical conditioning for children and adolescents with asthma.

## *BLIND*

Seamons GR: *Swimming for the Blind.* Provo UT, Brigham Young University, 1966.

This book is written as a manual for parents, teachers, and community members in providing aquatic programs adapted for visually impaired individuals. Values and history of swimming for the blind are reviewed. The value of this book lies in the descriptive details of instructional, safety, and practical adaptations for this population. The author provides a solid base of realistic expectations for the person working with the visually impaired swimmer. Emphasis is placed on safety and on prevention of panic, to which this population is especially susceptible.

Originally a master's thesis, the book is presented clearly and logically, with practical suggestions interspersed with theory. I would recommend this text for people working exclusively with the visually impaired as well as for those who have visually impaired participants in their program.

### *Additional References:*

Cordellos H: *Aquatic Recreation for the Blind.* AAHPER, Information and Resource Center, BEH, 1976.

Belenky R: *A Swimming Program for Blind Children.* New York, American Foundation for the Blind, 1965.

## *CEREBRAL PALSY*

Harris SR: Neurodevelopmental treatment approach for teaching swimming to cerebral palsied children. *Phys Ther* 58:979-983, 1978.

A model swimming program for cerebral palsied children based on the underlying principles of the neurodevelopmental treatment approach is presented.

The program is divided into three sections: general pool skills, pool activities and skills for various categories of cerebral palsy, and functional skills which might be introduced in the pool setting, yet later might become useful skills on land. Swimming is considered a recreational and a therapeutic activity that can be a valuable adjunct to a regular therapy program. The value of hydrotherapy is discussed and the current literature pertaining to swimming programs for the physically disabled is critically reviewed.

## LEARNING DISABILITY

### Additional Reference:

Miles NR: *Swimming Techniques for Children with Learning Disabilities.* Chicago, Developmental Learning Materials, 1970.

## MENTAL RETARDATION

Council for National Cooperation in Aquatics and American Association for Health, Physical Education and Recreation. *A Practical Guide for Teaching the Mentally Retarded to Swim.* Washington DC, AAHPER, 1969.

A compilation of writings by a committee of professionals working with mentally retarded adults and children, the guide provides information for aquatic personnel that is both specific to programs for the mentally retarded as well as applicable to other types of aquatic programs. The theme of general information and educational methods for working with the mentally retarded (e.g., developmental and behavioral modification techniques), and the importance of a total program in which services are coordinated and transfer of learning is facilitated, extends through the book. Specific aquatic methods described include: multisensory techniques, sequential progression, water orientation, circuit training and stunts and games. Pool design specially adapted for the retarded and equipment adjuncts are also described.

The chapter devoted to organization and administration of aquatic programs is complete and extremely helpful. Emphasis is given to public relations and cooperation with the other settings in which the mentally retarded individual functions.

The importance of documentation is also considered in various programmatic aspects, e.g., justifying the program, demonstrating individual progress. As these two activities are often deficient or absent in actual practice, this emphasis is of utmost importance.

Generally, the book accomplishes its purpose and is presented in a clear and logical way. Although brief discussions on safety do occur throughout the book, the safety aspects of the program seem to be considered less important than methods. As a result, the emphasis on safety, for this population especially, seems inadequate. Organizational features for aquatic programs presented in the book are among the best available in the literature.

### Additional References:

Horvat M, Bishop P: Implementing aquatic instruction for severely and profoundly mentally retarded individuals. *J Phys Educ* Jan/Feb, 1981.

Mason C: Pool activities with the multiply handicapped child. *Nurs Mirror* 25:50-52, 1975.

### MUSCULAR DYSTROPHY

Adams MA, Chandler LS: Effects of physical therapy program on vital capacity of patients with muscular dystrophy. *Phys Ther* 54: 494-496, 1974.

A combined program of swimming and intermittent positive pressure breathing therapy (IPPB) was added to the regular ongoing physical and occupational therapy programs for three boys, ages 11, 13, and 15, with diagnoses of Duchenne's muscular dystrophy. During Phase One of the treatment program, two 30-minute sessions of swimming and one session of IPPB were instituted each week. The swimming program emphasized breathing activities, such as underwater breath-holding and bobbing. During Phase Two, the swimming program continued twice weekly and the IPPB was increased to two sessions each week. During Phase Three, the swimming program was increased to four 20-minute sessions each week. The entire study lasted 11 months.

Consistent increases in vital capacity were shown during each of the three treatment phases for two of the boys. The third boy showed increases during Phases One and Three and a plateau (no change) during Phase Two. In all but one instance, vital capacity dropped off during the vacation periods between phases when no treatment was given.

This pilot study provides tentative support to the effectiveness of swimming and IPPB therapy in increasing or maintaining vital capacity in boys with Duchenne's muscular dystrophy. Limitations of the study include the small sample size, the failure to record repeated baseline measures, and the failure to report interobserver reliability data for the spirometer recordings. Also, the dependent measures apparently were taken by individuals who were aware of the phase of treatment in which the subjects were involved at the time, thus creating an expectancy bias.

### Additional Reference:

Gibbons A: Introducing the muscular dystrophy to the water. *Br J Phys Educ* 3(4): 51-53, 1972.

### SPINA BIFIDA

Dowrick PW, Dove C: The use of self-modeling to improve the swimming performance of spina bifida children. *J App Behav Anal* 13: 51-56, 1980.

A multiple baseline design across three subjects with myelomeningocele, aged 5 to 10 years, was used to evaluate the effectiveness of self-modeling on improving swimming performance. For purposes of this study, self-modeling was defined as "the behavioral change that results from the repeated observation of oneself on videotapes that show only desired target behaviors." Thirty-five behaviors related to independence in swimming were compiled to make up a "Water Confidence Behaviors Checklist." These water skill behaviors were observed and recorded on the checklist by a trained observer during each phase of the study. Interobserver reliability measures were taken later based on videotapes of the swim program. Observers were blind to the phase of treatment in which each child was involved.

Four videotapes were made during the initial observation session. Film X was three minutes long and showed all three children in the water demonstrating skills which were easily within their capabilities. Films A, B, and C were the "self-model" films; one film was made of each child performing those skills which were more advanced than their routine checklist skills. Each of these films was edited to remove any behaviors representing anxiety or distress on the part of the child.

During the baseline phase of the study, each child viewed Film X three times weekly, immediately prior to the swimming sessions. During the third week of the study, Child 1 was shown Film A (his self-modeling film) while the other two children continued to see Film X. Film B was similarly introduced for Child 2 during the fifth week of the study. Film C was introduced to Child 3 during the seventh week. Each phase of treatment lasted two weeks. After eight weeks, a new self-modeling film showing more advanced swimming skills was made for Child 1 (Film A') and the films for the other two children were discontinued. After three weeks, an even more advanced film was made (Film A'') and it was shown during the final three weeks of the study to Child 1.

Performance on the checklist improved for each child immediately following the introduction of the self-modeling film, then began to plateau. For Child 1, performance improved immediately following the introduction of Films A' and A'' while the performance of the other two children remained relatively constant. Both the observers and swimming instructors were blind to the phase of treatment in which each child was involved. This well-controlled study supports the use of self-modeling videotapes in improving swimming behavior in children with myelomeningocele. The authors speculate that this visual intervention strategy may be particularly appropriate for the type of child who lacks sensory information in the lower extremities, such as the child with myelomeningocele.

## INFANT SWIMMING PROGRAMS

### Additional References:

Ankeney J: *Any Child Can Swim.* Chicago, Contemporary Books, 1979.

Barnett H: Teaching infants to swim. *Educ Unlimited* 2(1):18-19, 1980.

Hutinger PL, Donsbach P: Water Activities to Enhance Development for Handicapped and High Risk Infants. Baby Buggy Paper #121. BEH, Washington, DC.

Prudden B: *Your Baby Can Swim.* New York, Readers Digest Press, 1974.

## FILMS

*Focus on Ability.* American Red Cross, Washington, DC, Stock #321604 (20 min.).

*Splash.* Documentary Films, 3217 Trout Gulch Rd, Aptos, CA 95003 (20 min., 16mm).

*Water Free.* International Rehabilitation Film Review Library, 20 W 40th St, New York, NY 10018 (35 min., 16mm).